Selfie-Facing

Analog Musings In A Digital World

John Branning

Selfie-Facing

Analog Musings in a Digital World

Paperback Edition: September 2017
Pusillanimous Books

www.JohnBranning.com

ISBN 978-0-9970773-2-2

Contents

Notes on the Paperback Version

The paperback version of this book

Is something at which I trust you'll take a look.

Containing a bevy of humorous screeds

It's something you'll find entertaining, indeed.

"What's different twixt this and the e-book?" you ask.

Fair question; I took the time for several tasks.

I fixed a few typos and changed a few words,

Took out a few entries that were for the birds.

But now, in their places, I've added two different.

They're short, to the point, and I trust not vociferent.

I hope it's now better, at least not made worse.

But maybe it is since I wrote this in verse.

-- September 2017

Preface

My father was fond of saying, "If you can't find something, turn the rock over. If you still can't find it, turn the rock over again." To this day, I still don't know what he meant and wish he'd spent less time obsessing over rocks and more time playing catch with me.

Other than my father's words of… let's call it "wisdom" for the time being, the rest of this book is filled with words of my own. Well, not words of my own – I mean, I use words that other people also make use of. Let me try again: the remainder of the book is comprised of original essays. Wait, that's not accurate, either – you'll also find some entries where I offer my own comments in response to quotes or observations generated by other word-users. Let's say somewhere between 80 – 85% of what you'll read from here on out can be considered "original." I'll adjust the price of the book accordingly to reflect this.

These pieces first appeared in my blog, *Facts Optional.* I've been writing since 2012 (well, I've been writing since I was about age three, but here I'm referring to the blog), focusing mostly on autobiographical snippets (generally pointing out my failings as a human being; lots of source material to draw from). I also love to write about the complexities of the English language, which I generally do in a way that also points out my failings as a human being, or at least that I failed English in high school. And then there are my aforementioned comments regarding what others have said, which I already mentioned in the previous paragraph and so let me adjust my assessment of original content here down to 75 – 79%.

Perhaps at this point I should wrap up the preface and let you get on with the remaining pages, if I haven't managed to put you off. A few family members, friends and acquaintances are on a distro list and have been receiving links to these columns via email. Those emails typically have a brief introduction to the linked column and I'm including them here at no extra charge to you (they'll be in italics when they feel like showing up). I trust you'll find at least a few moments of amusement as you meander through this book.

As my father often said… nope, I won't repeat myself again.

-- Winthrop, ME   November 2015

It's Snow Trouble

I took Driver's Ed together with my best friend of 40+ years, Bert. He has become a skilled wheelsman who regularly competes in sports car events at challenging road courses.

I once ripped the front bumper off our car while backing out of a parking space.

They say a journey of a thousand miles begins with but a single step.

We are stuck in a fucking snowbank in our driveway.

Let me back up; no, wait -- that's what got us into this predicament in the first place. Our driveway at the lake house has something of a steep drop right where you pull in. Entering -- it's a gas (no pun intended). When Carol isn't in the car with me I fly-y-y down the driveway as fast as I can; it's like being on a roller coaster for a few seconds. The turn is so sharp off the dirt road threading through our community that it's easy to miss seeing the driveway altogether, which adds to our sense of privacy and seclusion even though we have neighbors just yards away.

Exiting out of the driveway, however, is a different story. If it's dry, not much of a problem -- but if it's wet from rain, or leaves are covering the entrance, or -- as we just learned -- it has recently snowed almost a foot and the guy we hired to plow the driveway has managed to pack what didn't get pushed to the sides down so tightly that it's slick, that presents a challenge and it's not as much fun, whether Carol is in the car with me or not.

After our snowy weekend visit, with the driveway cleared by the afore-mentioned plow dude, we started the drive home. I put our trusty Highlander into low gear and clicked on the "ECT SNOW" setting which, after I've read the owner's manual, I now know reduces the transmission into an even lower setting and in this case got it down to something in the crawling-on-knees-and-elbows-for-traction range. We headed up the driveway, sliding a bit, and as we reached the precipice we... stopped moving forward. Tires began spinning, so I applied the brakes and backed up a few yards to try again. Up, up, up -- but not all the way. I now thought it would be best to return to the flat area near the house where we park and take a longer, faster run at it. I backed up the car in a straight line -- which was unfortunate since the driveway has a pronounced curve. Before I realized my error, I'd managed to back too close to one edge and into a pile of snow two feet deep. Now the entire driver's side was mired in the snowbank. I tried rocking the car to break it loose - no dice. I decided I needed to shovel out the snow surrounding the tires and side of the car. I went to open my door, which budged all of two inches since I'd also managed to sidle up against a row of saplings, effectively barricading me from exiting. After Carol daintily stepped from the passenger seat, I nimbly slid over the center console, managing to only slightly herniate myself, and gallantly stumbled out of the vehicle.

I walked back toward the house to retrieve the snow shovel and began to clear the area. After 10 minutes' worth of shoveling, rocking, shoveling, rocking, shoveling and finally pushing, Carol drove the car free from its packed-snow confinement (I mean, she didn't do all of that -- I was the source of the shoveling and provided a gonad-popping push). I guided her back down the driveway and wisely opted to leave her behind the wheel as we made our latest attempt to escape. She stomped on the gas like it was my manhood and we accelerated closer and closer to the entrance... flying over that ridge like two people in an SUV in low gear when one of them is a humiliated husband.

Now, it isn't like Carol's never gotten stuck in the snow. In fact, her story is a doozy -- but I won't recount it here out of respect for her. And my remaining testicle.

Artistic Lozenge

I'm a painter (of interior and exterior surfaces).

I like to draw (attention to myself).

I'm a master of technique (for getting the last little bit of toothpaste out of the tube).

I recently became a patron of one of Boston's leading art museums. I will admit to misunderstanding the terms of membership; I thought in exchange for my donation I'd be allowed to exhibit art works of my own making. However, I was mistaken and the very nice security guard explained it all to me as I was being taken away in handcuffs.

Some weeks after joining, I received an emailed invitation to the opening of a new exhibition. I was hoping this would be performance art and therefore involve some degree of nudity, but alas – the exhibition was largely comprised of paintings and drawings along with works in other media. While I believe many of the abstract figures were portrayed as nude or nearly so, it didn't have quite the sense of... accessibility I was anticipating. Regardless, the art work could best be described as... well, rather than my fumbling for words, here's a quote from the curator's catalog notes regarding one assemblage of multiple images:

- "Taken together, they form an oblique and inconclusive narrative."

I wrote that down -- "an oblique and inconclusive narrative." If being oblique and inconclusive are considered artistic qualities, then I am at least 90% of the way to setting foot back in that museum with no need for handcuffs to make a further appearance. Except as part of my "performance piece."

As many modern artists now seem to do, this one branched beyond her original mode of expression to create in other formats. Among the newer works were several animations made on an iPhone or iPad using a drawing program. What a co-ink-ee-dink! I have also made animations -- mine on a pad of Post-It notes -- usually sketches of an ever-enlarging part of the human anatomy that convey a brooding sense of eroticism and immaturity. Working in pencil, ballpoint or Sharpie, when viewed as part of a collection these images form a narrative that is neither oblique nor inconclusive -- they are clearly a penis getting bigger and bigger. The fact that this expansiveness requires the use of "flipping," the use of the viewer's hands to manipulate and display, is a clever commentary on the concept of auto-eroticism in our overtly-sexualized society, as well as indicative of the fact that I don't have enough to do at work.

I like contemporary art, I really do. We've been to shows that were absolutely thrilling at this same museum, along with MassMOCA, Dia:Beacon, the Hirschhorn and other galleries. While I may not have admired the craft, inspiration or intent of this artist's work as deeply as others I have seen, I surely was impressed with the cold beer and cheese board offered at the reception. And who knows? Maybe the alcohol and dairy products were artistic expressions utilizing yet more new media which, when taken together, formed another oblique and inconclusive narrative.

Or, in my case, intestinal bloating.

I'm Such an Idiom

You know what they say -- put 100 monkeys in a room with typewriters and eventually they'll come up with Shakespeare.

Here's what I came up with all by myself.

A journey of a thousand miles begins with but a single step. It ends with your significant other refusing to speak to you and flying home early.

Early to bed and early to rise works only if you don't have upstairs neighbors.

Hope for the best, prepare for the worst. That's why I tell my wife our dinner reservation is at 7:00 when it's really at 7:30.

Too many cooks spoil the broth. Hence, canned soup.

Bad news travels fast. Who told you we're coming to visit for the holidays?

Clothes don't make the man. Children in third-world countries make the clothes.

He who laughs last never sees the angry fist coming his way.

The way to a man's heart is through his stomach. At least, that's what my cardiologist billed me for.

A clear conscience is a soft pillow. I haven't slept well in months.

A soft answer turneth away wrath, but grievous words stir up anger. I'm angry that I don't know what the word "grievous" meaneth.

A wise man makes his own decisions, an ignorant man follows the public opinion. What do the rest of you think?

Flattery makes friends and truth makes enemies, so please ask someone else to tell you how you look in that outfit.

Give a man a fish, and he'll eat for a day. Teach him how to fish and he'll eat forever. He'll also be gone every weekend.

How wrong it is for a woman to expect the man to build the world she wants, rather than to create it herself. But I forget to empty the dishwasher one lousy time...

Actions speak louder than words. I said, "ACTIONS SPEAK LOUDER THAN WORDS."

Don't walk in front of me, I may not follow / Don't walk behind me, I may not lead / Just walk beside me and be my friend / But enough with the talking already.

The first half of our lives are ruined by our parents, and the second half by our children. The third half of our lives are ruined by our mathematicians.

No man is a failure who is enjoying life. Are we out of beer again?

Fools rush in where angels fear to tread. I'll catch up with you in a few minutes.

Whom we love best, to them we can say least. That's why the missus and I aren't on speaking terms.

Bucking Bronchi

I know it's a cliché this time of year to say "Everyone is sick" or "Something's going around" -- but hasn't that truly been the case with this endless winter?

Hoping this finds you healthy or at least recovering.

I'm recovering from a bout of bronchitis. I was about to say it hit me like a ton of bricks, but then it occurred to me it's probably just as bad to get hit by one brick as a ton of them. In fact, a ton may be preferable; you'd be unlikely to survive the onslaught and your suffering would be over quickly. However, if someone took a ton of bricks and hurled them at you one at a time, that might be worse than just one to the noggin or left nut or right shin or wherever it landed.

I'm pretty sure my wife regifted me with the bronchitis she'd been fighting off (should have thrown a brick at it) for the prior week and a half. Carol doesn't get sick often but when she does, she puts her all into it. Coughing, wheezing, sneezing, sleeplessness, kvetching... there's your million-dollar idea right there: a version of Sudafed that eliminates cough, congestion and kvetching. I put on my good-husband hat and made tea, warmed soup, brought tissues, expressed empathy. But what I could NOT bear to do was respond every time Carol blew her nose and then went, "Ugh... look at this!" I know what phlegm looks like and don't need any reminders. Have you seen the TV commercial where some poor woman is being chased down the street by a giant snot monster? "At the first sign of a cold, take --." Believe me, if you think a giant snot monster is pursuing you, you're well past the first sign of a cold and deep into feverish hallucinations and possibly early-onset dementia.

Anyway, after tending to the missus I thought I'd dodged a bullet (brick?) since I didn't seem to be coming down with anything myself. But about 10 days after wifey's first symptoms, I suddenly became congested and starting coughing and had the worst sore throat I could remember -- it felt like I'd tried to swallow a broken coffee mug that had lodged mid-gullet. For a few days I alternated between staying home and going into work; I flattered myself into thinking my presence was required for some meetings but, based on the terrified looks of the other attendees when they saw my condition, that assessment may have been erroneous. I tried to speak at one session and what came out of my mouth was a sound so low, guttural and primal that all the birds, rodents and feral cats living in downtown Boston began to stampede toward the Berkshires as if they'd heard the early off-shore rumblings of an approaching tsunami and were seeking refuge on higher ground.

Surprisingly there was a brief plus side to my ailment. One of the days I dragged myself into work I attempted to return a greeting from a co-worker; while it was obvious that I was ailing she said my voice sounded "sexy." I guess I did sound a little like Barry White if you could imagine him speaking immediately after biting his own tongue. Flash forward a week and a half and I ran into the same co-worker again; she asked if I was feeling better and I replied I was, albeit still getting over it. She said, "Well, you still sound a little sexy." Now I felt belittled and so desperately wanted to recover whatever elusive quality had rendered me full-on sexy mere days before that I considered throwing away the remainder of my supply of Mucinex.

As I type this, two full weeks after symptoms first appeared, I'm still experiencing the occasional chest-rattling cough and interrupting any interaction lasting more than 90 seconds with a nose-blow. But as much as I complain, Carol's had it worse -- toughing it out at work but exhausted when she gets home. Last night she was in bed by 8:30. Almost 14 hours later and she's still sleeping, so let me wrap this up and see if I can rouse her. Now, where's that brick?

Stinkin' Thinkin'

Sometimes I have a thought. Usually I shouldn't have bothered.

I asked my wife if she'd like to try a new position. She readily agreed, and now no longer endorses a carbon tax as the most economically efficient means to convey crucial price signals that spur emissions-reducing investments.

Instead of parallel parking, I tried perpendicular parking. On the plus side, it was much easier to pull into the space. On the negative side, I had a bitch of a time getting my purchases in the trunk without getting ass-swiped by passing traffic.

Using a trampoline while cleaning the gutters isn't as much fun as you might imagine.

In the face of adversity, I adopted a different approach to my nemesis and tried killing him with kindness. It didn't change the district attorney's sentencing recommendation.

I tried putting the cart before the horse. Now I'm out one cart and one horse.

Trying to manage my time more effectively, I spent the first half-hour of my day reviewing my schedule. I was then fired for being 30 minutes late for work.

A turntable may work in a microwave, but not a VCR.

Believing laughter is the best medicine, I stopped taking my Lipitor. Want to see the scar from my bypass?

Embracing the belief that honesty is the best policy, the last time my wife asked, "Do these pants make me look fat?" I replied, "They sure do." In all honesty, I wish I hadn't said that.

Just because you sign up for direct deposit with your bank doesn't mean they'll let you walk into their vault unimpeded.

Have you ever wondered if you could save money by changing the oil in your car yourself? Well, not if you use Wesson.

Despite its name, never dance while using a jig saw.

You'd think people trying to diet would appreciate having the refrigerator duct-taped closed. You'd think wrong.

Clowns In My Coffee

Beer, pizza, ice cream, coffee - the four food groups. Coffee can make an appearance in at least three of them.

I'm always surprised when someone says they don't drink coffee. "I don't like the taste," "It's too bitter," "Caffeine makes me jumpy," and the worst excuse is, "I drink tea, it's better for you." The medicinal benefits of coffee are well-documented; primarily, it helps you stay awake late at night while you Google the symptoms of whatever is keeping you from getting to sleep.

We all know someone who is an indiscriminate coffee drinker; usually a guy (if only because this supposition makes subsequent pronoun selection easier) who will drink the most vile brew without any standards whatsoever: re-heated; sat around for hours and is now burned/cold; uses powdered creamer; drinks flavored coffee (coffee already comes in a flavor, it's "coffee-flavored"), and the most egregious offense -- he drinks coffee from Dunkin' Donuts.

I won't get into the whole Starbucks vs. DD debate. Both places have their supporters and detractors. I'll say only Dunkin' Donuts is aptly named because even a fresh cup tastes like someone already stuck a cruller in it.

My friend Bert introduced us to the joys of hyper-caffeination. For years we served him coffee that we thought was at least adequate, and he never complained. During one of his visits, I had to run an errand in the morning and when I got back, he and Carol were having breakfast. "BERT MADE ME A CUP OF COFFEE!!!" Carol explained. "HE USED FOUR SCOOPS FOR ONE CUP!!!" Ever since then, we brew it strong so Carol won't have to go through detox.

I've studied Bert's method and this is how he brews the "perfect cup:"

1. Grind whole beans just when you are ready to use them.

2. For a pot of coffee, use an entire bag of beans.

3. While waiting for the pot to finish, drive down to the coffee shop at the corner and order a double-espresso to tide you over.

4. Repeat.

Once I was so amped up after drinking coffee with Bert I went to the driving range and hit a golf ball 148 yards. That may not sound impressive until I mention I was using a putter.

A few years ago Carol and I went camping for the first and thank God only time, meeting up with her brother's family and friends of theirs in an upstate New York park. Other than us, they were all experienced campers and carried a plethora of specialized equipment to provide most of the comforts of home while stuck in the woods. Foremost among them was a massive kitchen set-up that unfolded from a container the size of a briefcase into an area large enough to hold a full contingent of pots and pans, cooking utensils, an electrical outlet, a stovetop and maybe even a convection oven. Starting early in the morning, it took quite a while to set up. It began raining in the midst of the task, so a covering was required to protect it. Brother-in-law and his friend wrestled with a massive tarp while the rest of us stood idle and watched. As the hours ticked by, I politely asked my sister-in-law if she was able to get some coffee going while the effort continued. She said that was possible and 15 minutes later Carol and I were enjoying our java. When we were finished, she asked how we liked it and we said "very much." She smiled and said, "Good! I bet you couldn't tell it was decaf, could you?" Without another word we excused ourselves, got in our car, left the campground and raced twenty minutes to the nearest McDonald's for a jolt of caffeine, pulling into the drive-thru just as the dreaded withdrawal headache began pounding at our temples. I love my sister-in-law but at that moment I wanted to drive back to the campground, dig a hole, throw her in it, and bury her underneath several cubic yards of freshly-ground decaffeinated coffee.

Since it's usually just the two of us most mornings, I make coffee for Carol and myself using the pour-over method favored by the most pretentious of the neighborhood gourmet coffee bars. Using freshly-ground beans, unbleached paper filters, a cone, and a Japanese water pot I splurged on so I can "control the pour," it's a labor-intensive, time-consuming process that is made worthwhile by the clear moral superiority of the outcome. It was particularly time-consuming once when I knocked over the cone, scattering the grounds all over the counter -- and then did exactly the same thing a second time after grinding more $15-a-pound beans. I finally got everything properly measured and aligned and poured, enabling me to fill my mug with the rich, aromatic, velvety brew. Then I knocked that one over as well, spilling steaming hot coffee all over the counter and most of my torso. Carol, surely feeling the effects of caffeine-deprivation, found this hilarious. I evened the score after cleaning up -- I made her a mug of coffee after surreptitiously changing the setting on the grinder, placing it on a fineness of "7" rather than the usual "6," which tipped it from "Auto-Drip" to "Espresso." Revenge is a drink best served bold. She sipped from her cup, completely unaware of my treachery. Sighing contentedly, she smiled at me and said, "THANKS FOR THE COFFEE, HONEY!!!"

Parenting Mistakes I *May* Have Made With Our Son

I should have told him that our potty-training activity to "point and shoot" at the Cheerios floating in the bowl was limited to just the bathroom.

There was probably a better answer when he asked, "Where did I come from?" than showing him the video his mom and I made on our wedding night.

Taking him at his word that "baby teeth can grow back" may have cost me an extra $480 in visits from the tooth fairy.

Like many young boys, he went through a phase where he wanted to "marry" his mother. Staging a "ceremony" with the two of them was a harmless way to work through that temporary infatuation, but I wish I hadn't agreed to the alimony and child support payments.

Just because he said all his friends were doing it, I really shouldn't have let him drive himself to school during second grade.

Telling him he was getting old enough to be responsible for cleaning up after himself was the right thing to do. However, giving approval to grab "whatever tools you need" was poor direction, which I realized after he used the pressure washer to tidy up his room.

I should have not relied on his say-so that being allowed to skip a grade meant he could stay home for the entire school year.

Telling him he was the "man of the house" when I went on a business trip was an effort to impart feelings of maturity and responsibility. I do I wish I'd spoken up when I came home and found a "For Sale By Owner" sign on the front lawn.

Giving him sparklers to celebrate the 4th of July and a bunny rabbit at Easter weren't all that risky -- but letting him fly to Cabo for Cinco de Mayo during 7th grade wasn't prudent.

I really should have insisted he change the parental control password on the TV remote back to the default setting. I missed an entire season of "The Sopranos" because of that.

Looking back on it now, he may have been trying to pull a fast one when he said it made perfect sense to let him download his essay on "The History of Plagiarism" directly from the Internet.

Just because he said all his friends were doing it, I really shouldn't have let him take his date to the prom in a helicopter.

I think he was being less than truthful when he said all the after-school jobs he sought required application fees and could I front him the cash?

I am also suspicious that travel for his senior class trip to Daytona Beach was not via "the space shuttle" and question what my $40,000 ended up really being used for.

Has anyone else heard of an online university program that requires enrollees to live in a dorm and be on a meal plan?

Just because he said all his friends were doing it, I really shouldn't have let him take out a million-dollar AD&D policy on me, since I could barely afford the premiums. Although I was flattered when, just this week, he expressed his thanks by servicing the brakes on my car.

--

One mistake I did not make was to collaborate with his mother on producing a loving, bright, funny and generous child. Upon reflection, it might have been poor judgment giving *that* kid up for adoption...

Ant Misbehavin'

An unusual discovery - if you use latex paint, once thoroughly dry it's possible to peel away the entire layer you applied to cover the original surface below.

Peeling off the painter's tape toward, rather than away from, where you painted is a good way to get this process underway.

Not recommended.

Well, we're back from another weekend at the lake and the fun just doesn't stop. Over the next few paragraphs we'll be reviewing:

- Terrifying warnings of fire and carbon monoxide poisoning

- Entomology

- Something fan-tastic

- Shoddy electrical work

- Shopping hints

AN ALARMING SITUATION

We arrived at the lake house last Saturday morning around 11am – and upon entering were immediately met with a shrieking smoke detector and digitally-recorded audio warnings of "Fire! Evacuate immediately! Carbon Monoxide detected! You have eight seconds left to live... seven seconds... six seconds..." I did what anyone would in that situation – pulled the 9-volt battery out of the offending smoke detector to silence it. However, since this is an interlocking system of three detectors and they run on house current (the battery is there as a fail-safe during power outages), removing the battery only added a new warning to the others: "Low battery power! Someone is fucking with me!" Realizing I'd have to completely shut it down, I removed the cover from the bleating unit and disconnected the white (neutral) wire. That did two things: 1) generated a spark sizable enough to actually ignite the house, and 2) set off a series of echoing cries from the other two interconnected detector-mates: "Power interruption! System integrity compromised! Comrade down! Medic! Where's that goddam medic? DEFCON One! I don't think he's going to make it! Will you make sure his girlfriend gets the letter he wrote her that's tucked in his battery compartment?"

I then did what anyone would in that situation – read the instruction manual. Based on the symptoms, the likely cause was a malfunctioning unit. The manual advised calling the "24-Hour National Service Hotline" to report the malfunction. I dialed the toll-free number and got – a busy signal. Repeatedly. Over a 20-minute period. Really? They either have too many malfunctioning units or too few inbound phone lines at this company.

Eventually I read through some of the other diagnostic steps and vacuumed in and around the hyperbolic detector, wired it back up and tested the system (resulting in yet another round of shrieking alarms and shouts of "Fire! Carbon Monoxide! Impending Doom!"). That seemed to settle everything down.

(Until 1:00 AM Sunday morning, when the same unit decided the house was on "Fire!" and advised us to run for the hills. I glared at it, and it then decided perhaps it had arrived at a too-hasty conclusion and apologized for waking us. All the units kept their yaps shut for the remainder of the weekend.)

WHAT'S BUGGING ME?

After resolving the issue with the smoke detectors, we dove back into ceiling painting and bathroom updating. Applying a new bead of caulk around the tub and shower was Job #1 for me – the previous owner appeared to have suffered the unexpected onset of Parkinson's when he last handled that task but valiantly kept at it; the old caulk was not so much "applied" as "smeared." It made for a tiring day, up and down ladders and more exertion than we normally experience while seated on the couch, so after a late dinner we were ready for bed.

Taking turns in the bathroom, I finished first and went upstairs. I turned on the bedside lamp to read while waiting for Carol. After a few minutes she entered the room and exclaimed, "OH MY GOD! LOOK AT THIS!" and pointed at the ceiling. There, attracted by the light, were approximately 5,286 moths, gnats and other winged creatures. We'd placed an a/c unit in the bedroom window temporarily since it was so warm over the holiday weekend, but thinking it wouldn't be remaining in that room long-term didn't bother to seal around it. This approach provided only a marginally-daunting challenge to the bugs who wanted to come inside for a visit. We led them out of the bedroom by turning on the hall light and turning off the bedroom light, then going downstairs and turning on the kitchen light and off the hall light and so gradually re-directed the swarm out onto the porch. We went back up to our bedroom, which was now nearly bug-free, and settled back under the covers. Our rest was interrupted only by the 1:00 AM warning of "Fire! Boils! Frogs! Murrain!" from that overly-diligent smoke detector located outside the bedroom.

After that refreshing sleep, we awoke to a sunny Sunday morning and went downstairs for breakfast. As she carried coffee into the dining room Carol exclaimed, "OH MY GOD! LOOK AT THIS!" On the carpet directly underneath an outlet box where we planned to install a ceiling fan was a pile of ants. Dead ants. Which, while we stood there watching, was added to by colony-mates coming out from the overhead opening with fallen comrades in their clutches who were dropped to the floor below.

We vacuumed up the pile and, within minutes, found a new pile taking its place. This activity continued for the remainder of the day. Google informs this is symptomatic of a carpenter ant invasion, so we've added "call exterminator" to our punch list. The pile of dead ants is known as a "frass," as in, "What did the frass-hole who sold us this place do to attract so many ants?" While we were initially shocked at the find, the ants' methodical activity and touching reverence shown for their dead were fascinating. And gross.

INELIGIBLE RECEIVER

Once the ant activity ceased (deceased?), we proceeded to put up a ceiling fan. I'd installed a similar unit in our Cambridge apartment a few years ago -- that job took me two weeks and three hours to complete. Let me explain: I'd gotten 30 minutes into the job and was flummoxed by the instructions, so left the partially-assembled fan hanging from a small hook overhead in our family room for many days until Carol deciphered the directions and got me back on track to then finish the task in another two and a half hours. This time, I noticed the instructions said the job was estimated to take only "120 minutes." Both fans included a remote-control unit, meaning it required wiring up the wazoo to connect the remote receiver to the household circuit and fan/light kit. One of the big challenges with the original installation was gingerly maneuvering the receiver to fit into a space that appeared to be far too small to house it without ripping all the wiring loose. Again – Carol came to the rescue, displaying exceptional manual dexterity and spatial awareness as she firmly shoved it into place.

After carefully wiring all the leads, I flipped to the next page in the instruction booklet, expecting the step where it told you to insert the receiver into the canopy. Instead, the instructions moved on to installation of the light kit, completely skipping what to do with the receiver. Well, that's one way to make the job an hour shorter... If we hadn't already been through the same process, that would have been the point at which I'd become flummoxed (perhaps you can tell I am often and easily flummoxed) and the swearing would commence. In all candor, I was a little disappointed I didn't get to the expletive-laden part of the install.

Carol climbed the ladder and again carefully smashed the receiver into place. I finished securing the canopy and installed the light kit. I placed the battery in the controller, flipped the wall switch, pressed the proper buttons on the remote and – nothing happened. Hooray – my opportunity to swear! Turned out there were two wall switches controlling that outlet and they both needed to be in the correct position for the fan to work. Once we had them aligned, the remote took over: the fan spun rapidly and noiselessly, sending a cooling breeze -- and a spray of ant carcasses -- across the living room.

I'LL FIXTURE YOU

By Monday the caulk and bathroom paint were dry and so it was time to install the toilet paper holder and towel bar on the wall, and the light fixture over the sink.

Toilet paper holder: holes from the previous paper holder don't line up with the new holder. This means drilling / spackling / repainting.

Towel bar: holes from the old towel bar are exactly the same distance apart as those required for the new towel bar.

Unfortunately, holes for the old bar are aligned horizontally and those for the new bar are aligned vertically. This means drilling / spackling / repainting.

Light fixture: I now notice that the old light fixture wasn't connected to an outlet box. Instead, the backing plate to the old fixture had been held in place with one screw driven into a stud, which was apparently sufficient to hold everything in place once assembled. This creates a conundrum with the new fixture, which clearly needs to be screwed to an outlet box in order to secure a center post to which the rest of the fixture is attached. This means carpentry / wiring / drilling / spackling / repainting / lots of swearing.

I thought of suggesting to Carol that, since we now lived right on a body of water, perhaps indoor plumbing wasn't essential? But then thought better of it.

HONE SHOPPING NETWORK

When deciding where to purchase home repair/remodeling supplies, people often base their choices on "reviews" or "ratings" or "best of..." lists. Don't do that – buy ALL the shit you need at whatever outlet is closest to the domicile you are rehabbing. We have receipts for purchases at Home Depot (three different locations), Lowe's, Ace Hardware, Target, Bed Bath & Beyond, T.J. Maxx, Marshall's, Christmas Tree Shops, and Big Lots! (I'm not excited about that one; the "!" is part of their name), Ocean State Job Lot (two locations, neither of which were located in the "Ocean State"), and 3 different furniture stores. We picked Home Depot because their brand of paint is supposed to be "Highest-Rated by a Leading Consumer Publication." Despite our coverage calculations we've been back two additional times to pick up more of the same custom colors (those are just the return trips for paint – I've lost count of the total number of trips for everything else). Carol kept saying, "They have a record of the paint we bought." When I pointed out that no one had ever asked for her: 1) name; 2) phone number; 3) address; 4) SSN, 5) birth date, 6) shoe size or 7) any other identifying information, she reconsidered and thought perhaps we would need to remember which paint we'd decided was "perfect" for which room(s). Two different ceiling paints, 5 different room colors, and who the hell can remember the difference between "eggshell" and "satin" finish? Ace Hardware is closest to our new address; their paint comes in just as many colors as any place else's and is also "Highest-Rated by a Leading Consumer Publication." I believe that publication is Highlights for Children.

The next time we're up there – if I see any more ants, I'll cry uncle.

Things I Don't Understand

I flew out to British Columbia this past weekend for a quick visit with college friends. I was sitting near the back of the plane and was surprised that many of the other passengers tried to rush for the front exit without letting the people in front of them collect their things and move out in an orderly fashion, row by row. I don't fly as much as I used to -- but when did that social convention change?

I had three ways to respond to this behavior:

1. *Ignore it.*

2. *Shake my head in disbelief.*

3. *Hook the trailing strap from their shoulder bags over the arm rest as they passed by me.*

If you chose "1" or "2" from the list above -- well, you don't know me very well, do you?

I paid a lot of money to see this movie, so why do they show me commercials before it starts?

Why do people stop dead in their tracks the moment they exit the jetway? Do they think the other passengers behind them have no place else to go?

Why do people make racist statements and then claim they're not racist? That's like if I jump into a pool and then say I wasn't expecting to get wet.

Why do people step into pedestrian walkways that are clearly displaying "DO NOT WALK" symbols, in front of oncoming traffic? And yet when they're behind the wheel they immediately honk if the car in front of them doesn't move the instant the light turns green?

Why do gas station pumps post signs prohibiting cellphone use so you're not distracted while using them, but have TV displays built in? Is this so you can see the breaking news report "Car Explodes!" while your vehicle is engulfed in flames?

Why do we plead "ignorance of the law" only when we're guilty of something? Does anyone ever win a lawsuit and then claim "I had no idea what was going on in the courtroom?"

Why do people at concerts engage in loud conversations while the band is playing? How would they like it if someone launched into a drum solo in the middle of their PowerPoint presentation at work?

Why do grocery stores sell motor oil? I wouldn't buy ground beef at AutoZone.

What kind of world do we live in that I even know who Kim Kardashian IS?

If your boss expects you to work at home in the evenings, why does she get upset if you nap at the office during the day?

Why do kids reply immediately to texts from their friends but when asked in-person to clean their rooms respond with, "... later?"

If we're descended from the apes then why can't I scamper up trees?

Why would anyone make an obscene gesture at another driver when they have no idea if there's a gun in that car?

Why do people ask if you have time to talk when you answer their calls? And why do you answer their calls if you don't?

Language-ing by the Pool

I have an uncanny knack for identifying typographical and grammatical errors in television ads, particularly those for legal services. After all, for years opponents of Obamacare anchored their fight to overturn it to what was claimed to be a typo — the distinction between "state" and "states." When writing legislation, one should be careful to states one's case more clearfully.

I've been speaking English my entire life (minus the first 18 months or so), and reading and writing it nearly as long -- and somehow only recently have I become aware of the "Oxford comma." I mean, I knew what it was, but I just didn't realize it was a part of punctuation that had this particular name attached to it, like "capital letters" and "missed my period." [And before we go any further here -- was the period in that last sentence supposed to be placed within or outside of the quotation marks? Just to be clear, I'm not talking about the "missed" period.]

Now it seems not a week goes by that some twit... er, I mean some tweet references the "Oxford comma," or a blog post or some other forum for lexicographic commentary. I'd heard of Oxford collars, and Oxford shoes, and the Oxford Press (where, I presume, one would have a shirt with an Oxford collar ironed). I do recall learning not to place a comma before the last item in a series. Said comma, when placed, is known as the Oxford comma. Are there names for other kinds of commas? The only other one I know by name is a "medically-induced comma," which is what language-obsessives are placed into after their participation in frenzied debates regarding the disregard of proper grammatical practices causes them to stroke out.

I won't rehash the two sides to the Oxford comma issue here since there are many other, more-learned, references one could Google if one were so inclined. Or more than one of you, if you can persuade your friend to join you in Googling. However, this kerfuffle has caused me to investigate what other rules of grammar, spelling and writing (or should that be "grammar, spelling, and writing"? or "grammar, spelling, and writing?") ...what was I saying? Oh yes -- here are some other grammatical rules with which I've recently become reacquainted with:

- "i" before "e," except after 3:00 PM.

- Don't leave a participle dangling; make a clean break from the relationship and then walk away.

- The plural of any singular noun ending in "y" is more than you'll ever need.

- "Who" and "Whom" are frequently confused for one another, but not as often now that "Whom" got her hair cut.

- "Lay" is an intransitive verb; "lie" is what I just told you.

- Proper use of "its" vs. "it's" can be easily resolved by reading your sentence out loud and substituting "it is" for whichever word you used. If the sentence sounds silly, try reading it again in your normal tone of voice.

- Should it be "between you and I" or "between you and me?" Sorry, honey -- I broke it off with you months ago; get over it. And take your participle with you.

- Context is often helpful when trying to determine which word is correct. For example, telling your sister-in-law "You've put on a *complement* of 20 pounds since I last saw you" would not be taken as a *compliment*.

- If you can count it, use "fewer." If you can't count it, then a spreadsheet is required.

- Some common phrases just confound all logic. As an example, you'll ask for "a pair of scissors," when you only want one scissor. The plural of "moose" is also "moose," which is why they so rarely come when called -- they're not sure which one of them you're talking to.

- A semi-colon is what many people are forced to use after a bowel resection.

- Did you know you should place a predicate pronoun after an infinitive? Me neither.

- "Hopefully" is a dangling modifier. Fortunately, the attendant will point it out before you leave the men's room.

Those of we whom are interested in the dynamics of the English language are familiar with The Elements of Style, which is often referred to as "Strunk and White" after it is two co-authors, some guy named Strunk and the editor E. B. White. Many years ago, I had the pleasure of speaking with the late Mr. White (in this context, late means "deceased" as opposed to "not on time." However, I am fairly certain I spoke with him before he ceased being.). I'll never forget what he said to me: "How did you get my phone number? Stop bothering me, for crisssakes. Your giving me a heart attack." I didn't have the strunk to tell him he'd mis-spoken; surely he meant to say, "Your giving *I* a heart attack."

Hopefully, upon all of you a similar impression I has made.

Moved to Tears

A few weeks ago on a Friday the high in Boston reached 99 degrees, the hottest day of the year so far (in fact, the hottest day of the 21st century to date in the Hub). What better day then could there possibly have been for us to move into our new apartment?

The moving crew arrived shortly before 8:00 am (only a balmy 89 at that time). We hired the same company that moved us from Boston to Cambridge four years ago; the high that day only reached 97 and we wanted to give this company a chance to top itself. Four strapping young men showed up, ranging from a mere 6' to a towering 6' 9." One of the lads was from Ireland, and the other three from Lithuania. The tallest, a blond and muscular hunk named Darius (at least, that's what it sounded like to us), spoke the least English (except for the guy from Ireland) and answered "Yes" to nearly every question Carol asked him: "Would you like a cold drink?" -- "Yes…" "How long have you been in this country?" -- "Yes…" "If I can get rid of my husband for a little while, will you have your way with me?" -- "Yes…" Shortly after his arrival, Carol sent me out to look for her high school diploma which she insisted was in the car and I was not to come back until I found it. Christ, I looked everywhere and no luck… I came back inside some time later and was sure she'd be mad at me, but she was smiling and didn't seem to mind at all despite the obvious flush on her face from the heat that day. She's such a doll!

The crew raced up and down two flights of stairs all morning long. I was impressed by their stamina (Carol agreed), so much so that I attempted one such sprint myself and spent the rest of the day hobbled and limping. Darius also had a bad knee (recovering from an ACL tear). Carol, being a physical therapist, graciously offered to examine him closely in another room and told me afterward that the injury hadn't slowed him down one bit. Remarkable! I guess they have some excellent surgeons back in the "old country."

After they packed all our belongings in the truck, it was time for a lunch break. Carol wanted these fellows to know how much she appreciated their efforts on this brutal day, so she suggested I go pick up lunch at a nearby Greek place. Even though it was just around the corner from our apartment, the walk there was challenging in the heat, plus I had to turn around and go back several times because Carol kept texting me to change their drink orders. Poor lads – I can only imagine how desperately they needed to slake their thirst that day.

After lunch we were ready to head to our new place and unload everything, so I told the crew, "It's time for you to do it all over again, backwards!" Right at that moment, Carol must have choked on a bit of her meal since she started coughing and turned beet red. I hopped in the car and Carol prudently suggested she'd ride in the back of the truck along with Darius in order to make sure nothing shifted during the brief trip to our new apartment. There was some mid-day traffic as we drove into the tunnel leading us to the highway, and I lost sight of the truck among the surge of other vehicles. I continued to drive to the new apartment and got there before the movers. I guess they must have hit another knot of traffic along the way, because it was a solid hour after my arrival before they showed up.

Our new place is smaller than the old one. While we've moved several pieces of furniture up to the lake, we still have a lot of stuff and it was quite a puzzle figuring out what would go where. I looked around and complained, "This can't possibly all fit in this tight space!" Carol and the crew got quite a chuckle from my outburst, with Carol replying, "Oh, you'd be surprised!" The crew found her response hilarious; I didn't get the joke but laughed along good-naturedly.

Again, the crew hustled like mad men, bringing up boxes faster than we could direct where to put them. The new place has two small porches, front and back – those quickly turned into storage areas for the overflow. At one point, I was actually blocked off in the back porch with boxes stacked all around me and no way to reach the door back into the apartment. I called out to Carol for nearly 45 minutes to come rescue me, but I guess she couldn't hear over the constant din of activity. It was actually the Irish lad who came along to let me out. I was quite frazzled by being trapped in the small space with no fresh air on such a hot day, yet he apparently found my experience amusing since he was laughing uproariously as he cleared a path back into the apartment.

Finally, some ten hours after getting started, all of our things were now in their new home. I'd planned to give the crew generous tips and had gone to the bank the day before to make sure I had enough cash on hand. However, Carol thoughtfully suggested that due to the conditions we should double the amount, so I went off in search of a bank which, since the neighborhood was largely unfamiliar to me, took quite a while. But I wasn't worried since Carol had told me not to rush; she'd keep the boys occupied until I made it back. I returned some time later to find everyone obviously exhausted from the day's vigorous activities. I handed out the tips, telling them they'd been worth every penny. Such a good-humored group of guys; they found that innocuous comment amusing as well! Carol was so appreciative of their hard work that she gave each fellow a lingering hug and warm kiss of thanks. She is just such an affectionate and caring person.

We are still unpacking; it's been a busy few weeks since the move and Carol has had to work more late nights than usual and comes home exhausted. Funnily enough, I saw Darius in the neighborhood several days after the move and mentioned that coincidence to Carol. She told me she was treating him for his ACL injury but, since he didn't have insurance in this country, had to sneak him in to her department after hours for massage and other touch therapies. She said he was responding very well but treatment would need to continue indefinitely. That woman is a saint, isn't she? Brings tears to my eyes...

Freedom of Depress

This was an actual item from the online version of the New York Times (both corrections for the same article):

Correction: January 10, 2014

An earlier version of this article misidentified the reporter. Marc S------ wrote that version of the article, not Kate Z------. Both wrote later versions.

Correction: January 10, 2014

An earlier version of this article misidentified the state where Andrew M. Cuomo is governor. It is New York, not New Jersey.

I find it amusing that the "paper of record" is unsure of: a) who their reporters are, and b) who's the governor of the state where they are based.

I guess this puts the "ass" in "media bi-ass."

Correction: January 11, 2014

An earlier version of this article misidentified the capital of the United States. It is Washington, D.C., not Hooterville.

Correction: January 10, 2014

An earlier version of this article misidentified my wife. She is Carol, not Kate Upton.

Correction: January 9, 2014

An earlier version of this article misidentified the sum of 2 + 2. It is 4, not "about 4."

Correction: January 8, 2014

An earlier version of this article misidentified my son. He is Joshua, not "that shit-head."

Correction: January 7, 2014

An earlier version of this article mischaracterized watching "Duck Dynasty" as a "complete waste of time." It is more accurately characterized as a "complete fucking waste of time."

Correction: January 6, 2014

An earlier version of this article misdirected you to look over there while I removed twenty dollars from your wallet.

Correction: January 5, 2014

A photograph accompanying an earlier version of this article misidentified the person pictured as the actor George Clooney. It was in fact my "selfie."

Correction: January 4, 2014

An earlier version of this article misidentified you as deceased. More accurately, you are "dead to me now."

Correction: January 3, 2014

An earlier version of this article inappropriately rhymed "Piscataway" with "He went over there."

Correction: January 2, 2014

An earlier version of this article may have left you with the impression that I know what I'm talking about.

Correction: January 1, 2014

An earlier version of this article mischaracterized life as worth living.

The Princess and the Pee Stain

Carol came downstairs this morning berating me, since she'd slipped on the path of rose petals I'd strewn along the steps to welcome her to the new day. You try to do something nice for someone... To her credit, she quickly got over her pique, stepping into my outstretched arms for a good morning hug. I then noticed she was wearing her pajamas inside-out. While I considered it unlikely that she'd had a romp with someone else while I was sleeping undisturbed (thanks to my earplugs) during the night, I did think it prudent to ask why her clothing was so arranged.

"It's because my skin is so sensitive -- if I sleep with my pj's right-side out, the inside seams leave marks." I said that sounded ridiculous, so to prove her point Carol removed her pajama top to show me where she still had marks from not reversing her bedclothes before turning in several nights before. At least, I think that's what her intention was but I was focused on, shall we say, other desirable parts of her body that were now revealed.

Once I came out of my reverie, I saw reddened creases under her arms and along her sides. I offered a look of concern -- briefly -- and then, as is my wont, started in with the wisecracks:

"If they made corduroy pajamas, you'd wake up looking like a Ruffles potato chip."

"If I'd known you were that sensitive, I wouldn't have told you how stupid I thought *Under the Tuscan Sun* was."

"The only other time something left that much of a painful impression on you was when you found out one of your yoga teachers was a Trump supporter."

I was coming up with some pretty funny zingers... well -- I was laughing. Carol calmly went into the kitchen to get herself a cup of coffee while I continued riffing. When she returned, she took a sip from her cup and then said, "At least I don't have pee stains on the front of my pants when I come out from the bathroom."

A morning that only moments before had been warmed by mirth now turned icy cold. Carol's comment had wounded my soul, and I quickly ran through the Five Stages of Grief it had caused me:

Denial -- "I do not come out of the bathroom with pee stains on the front of my pants!"

Anger -- "I can't believe you would make fun of my incontinence issues."

Bargaining -- "If you'll lay off the insults, I'll go to another one of those idiotic 'mindfulness' seminars with you, OK?"

Depression -- "You have no idea how much I'm on edge every time I exit a public washroom."

Acceptance -- "I guess I could think about trying some 'adult' underwear..."

As I started to come out of my funk, I noticed Carol was snickering. "What's so amusing?" I asked. She finished sipping from her cup before responding, "Look who's sensitive now! I guess I'm not the only one with 'thin skin' around here."

After a few moments of contemplation, I forced a smile and said fair was fair -- I'd landed the first blow, and she had only counter-punched in return. I apologized for my insensitive response to her dermatologic dismay, offering to make amends by going upstairs to strip the bed and remake it with fresh sheets while she relaxed over the rest of her coffee. She said that was very nice of me, taking a seat at the dining room table while I sprinted up to the bedroom to complete my penance.

It will be interesting tomorrow morning to see what her skin looks like after spending a night sleeping on luxurious, 400-thread-count Egyptian cotton sheets -- under which, on her side of the mattress, I slid a piece of corrugated cardboard. Rest well, Your Highness!

Don't Ass, Don't Yell

... and when the doctor goes to sign the chart, he pulls a rectal thermometer from his jacket pocket. "Oh, my!" he says...

Considering changing the name of the blog to "Punchline Optional." Email me if you want to hear the rest of that joke.

Certainly you remember the now-abandoned "Don't Ask, Don't Tell" policy in our military, which was essentially a way for our government to stick its fingers in its ears and go "LA-LA-LA-LA-LA!" whenever the subject of a soldier's sexual orientation came up.

Would that I'd be so diffident when it comes to the subject of my recent colonoscopy -- so get those fingers in place now.

I'm sure you're familiar with the concept of a colonoscopy, but have you actually had one? The CDC (part of the same government that came up with "LA-LA-LA-LA-LA!") recommends regular screenings for men and women, regardless of sexual orientation, starting at age 50. Why age 50? It's an implied half-way point of life, so does this mean the government thinks I'm going to live to be 100? That comes as a surprise to me. A recent article says half of all babies born today will live to be 100. The other half will live to have regular colonoscopies performed on them.

Everyone who's had a colonoscopy, or is familiar with the procedure, knows that "the prep" is the worst part of the process. You can't eat any solid foods the day before; clear liquids and Jell-O only. Then, that evening, you drink 4 liters of a "bowel cleansing" solution and after a while you run repeatedly to the bathroom to, as your mother used to say, "make." (The solution comes in two flavors: pineapple and "regular." My pharmacy provided me with the "regular" -- once reconstituted I recognized the taste as Pine-Sol.) Over the course of several hours you'll make at least a dozen trips to the bathroom. The solution turns your gastrointestinal tract into a garden hose, with the spigot all the way open. I've already provided too much detail here and so will leave this section of our narrative with the words I shared with a friend - "I'm glad that shit's over."

The actual procedure is almost anti-climactic, since they give you the good drugs just before starting to poke around in your hoo-hah and actual memories of this hideous violation are almost non-existent. I remember being a little nervous when the anesthesiologist told me he'd be using Propofol, the drug that became infamous due to its association with Michael Jackson's death, but ironically my anxiety was relieved by the administration of that very drug. During a prior colonoscopy I was given Versed which, as a layperson, I thought was pretty freakin' awesome. However, that drug will induce only "conscious sedation" versus the state of "deep sedation" Propofol provides. Conscious sedation is defined as when "the patient responds purposefully to verbal command," and deep sedation is when "the patient cannot be easily aroused, but responds purposefully following repeated or painful stimulation." As it relates to my procedure, under conscious sedation the gastroenterologist says, "John, please move your hips forward. John, can you move your hips forward?" and I dreamily move my hips forward. Under deep sedation, the gastroenterologist goes, "John (pokes with probe), move! (Pokes) Move! (POKES) MOVE, DAMMIT!"

By the way -- it just struck me that the word "enter" is found in the middle of "gastroenterologist." That's kinda funny.

After the procedure ended (!), I was moved to a recovery room that I call the "Man Cave" since the nurse told me it was perfectly acceptable to fart as much as I felt necessary. I did so, and then some. As I awaited discharge (here by which I mean permission to leave the hospital), another patient was moved into the space next to me. I overheard some conversation between a nurse and doctor (HIPAA violation!) that the gentleman had been brought back for a second attempt at the procedure since, during his appointment the day before, he "wasn't clean." As there was also discussion about his need for a Vietnamese interpreter, I presumed they hadn't been referring to his sense of humor. I can only imagine what that experience must be like for the colon team... the patient's been sedated, buttocks aligned just so, the doctor slips the scope in and WHAT THE FU...?!?! Maybe due to the language barrier this guy thought he only needed to gargle with the prep solution.

Anyway, my results were good and I won't have to repeat the process for another five years. I'm referring to the colonoscopy -- I intend to maintain my usual pace of farting. If you haven't already, this is where I'd recommend you stick your fingers in your ears, and maybe you should also step out of the room.

Reasoned Heedings

I'm not really this crabby - just trying to present a "fair and balanced" view of the holiday.

A Merry and a Happy to all!

I do not like Christmas, don't like it at all.
Won't do any shopping, won't go to the mall.

It's lost what little meaning it had to me
Amidst all the bombast and hyperbole.

White Santas, Black Santas - are any Chinese?
How do kids choose from among all of these?

Pressure to spend precious coin I don't own
Just to get a new juicer, or machine for lawn mowin'.

The rush and the pressure, the crowds and the travel
Cause what little composure I have to unravel.

They say there's a war on, but where is the battle?
I'm tired of hearing the commenters prattle.

Some are so offended if offered wrong greeting
They don't seem to realize the season is fleeting.

The New Year comes quickly, then all's back to normal.
Bonhomie is gone -- all are back to bein' horrible.

The traffic, the parties, the food and the drink
It's all just too much, pushing me to the brink.

I can't stand the music, or anything "jingle."
And yet every year there's a new Christmas single.

They cost more on iTunes than when they were plastic.
The lyrics are dopey, the rhythms are spastic.

I'm tired of Christmas - it's shallow and phony.
And once again no one has brought me a pony.

Muse Once and Dispose of Immediately

As many of you know, my mind often wanders. Why, just the other day

I'm curious about what happens when:

- A frog gets warts?

- You and the other guy blink at the same time?

- Someone says "I could care less" and then actually does?

- Your sneakers make noise?

- You tell someone they are "as beautiful as the day is long" during the Winter Solstice?

- You trip and fall ass over teakettle at a Starbucks?

- You find out the person you accused of telling a "bald-faced lie" has alopecia?

- You wake up in the hospital and find out living really isn't that easy with eyes closed?

- You face gets stuck that way, and everyone says you look great?

- You become the "Big Cheese" but you're lactose-intolerant?

- You dump Xanax in a lake? (Answer: You reduce surface tension.)

- The forecast calls for a 50% chance of rain? Does that mean it's equally as likely that we'll be invaded by aliens on that day?

- A fish drops out of school?

- You try to paddle someone else's canoe?

- You get excited your wife mentions she'd like a three-way, and then you realize she's talking about a light bulb?

- You are dyslexic and ask for persimmon to go to the bathroom?

- You remember where you put your car keys but forget where you wanted to go?

Tightening the Neuse

This one meanders a bit, so grab a cup of coffee or perhaps a stiff drink (as I had while scribing) before getting started.

I was watching an old movie the other evening and heard a character describe herself as an "entrepreneuse." Never having heard the word before, along with the plummy accent the actress affected for the role, it took a moment for the term to register. Once my brain caught up with my ears, I realized how she had identified her vocation: a female entrepreneur. In today's world we strive to avoid gender-specific titles, not only to sidestep accusations of sexism but because anything a man can do, a woman can do while going backwards and wearing heels. Which, in my opinion, should prevent women from becoming Uber drivers but government regulations insist otherwise.

Performers such as Amy Schumer and Sarah Silverman are today referred to as "comedians" rather than "comediennes." When I was growing up, variety programs like The Ed Sullivan Show and The Hollywood Palace were popular on TV. Each week's installment was likely to feature a woman introduced as a "comedienne:" Phyllis Diller, Totie Fields, Joan Rivers. While Diller and Fields are long gone, Joan Rivers' career lasted right up until her untimely death in 2014, by which time she was called just a "plastic surgery nightmare" -- every bit the equal of men like Kenny Rogers or Carrot Top.

I racked my brain to come up with all the other "-euse" words I could recall:

Chanteuse: A woman who really can't sing yet appears in a nightclub where smoking is still permitted. Historically, the term is most closely associated with French performer Édith Pilaf, an international sensation best known for her timeless hit, "La Vie en Arroz."

Chartreuse: a truly hideous color unless your wife is wearing something featuring it, in which case it's best acknowledged as "retro."

Pampleneuse: a female grapefruit

Perhaps I didn't so much rack my brain as give it a gentle squeeze.

The movie I was watching was *The Story of Vernon and Irene Castle*, released in 1939 and starring Fred Astaire and Ginger Rogers. The Castles were essentially the Astaire and Rogers of their day; a husband and wife team who introduced the tango, among other dances, to European and American audiences. The couple was popular before the advent of movies as we know them today (or even as they were known in '39), so they gained fame performing in ballroom settings and theater stages. Their signature dance was known as the "Castle Walk," which was recreated in the movie and can best be described as a man and woman, both named "Castle," walking around the perimeter of the dance floor. Occasionally they would break into a sideways skip before bringing it down a notch and returning to walking. Inexplicably, this became an international sensation, with society-types quickly adopting the dance because it relieved them from anything requiring coordination or rhythm or the need to actually, you know -- dance. But back in 1910s the Castles were a big freaking deal, becoming superstars not only for their routines but also lending their names to dance studios, nightclubs (where maybe they met a chanteuse or teu), footwear and other fashionable clothing items. Irene was also the Jennifer Aniston of her times; she got a short trim that came to be known as the "Castle Bob" and women across the country flocked to hair salons to have their tresses so coiffed, coming home to show off the style to spouses who, just as today, didn't notice anything different.

The film ended on a tragic note, which at first I thought was dramatized for cinematic input but learned was true -- Vernon Castle, who was English by birth, enlisted in the Royal Flying Corps during WWI (receiving the Croix de Guerre for his actions in combat) and died in a plane crash in 1918 while serving as a flight instructor. He essentially sacrificed himself because he always insisted on taking the front seat in a Jenny biplane's cockpit so his trainees would be safer sitting in the rear. To avoid a mid-air collision with another cadet's plane, he stalled while attempting a steep climb and crashed, killing him but leaving his rear-seat student with only minor injuries. While I'm sure this was tragic in real life, the cinematic version was made unintentionally hilarious due to the flying recreations using then-state of the art special effects; i.e., model planes "flying" via the use of hidden sticks and the dramatic "crash" looking as though the model was dropped into one of those dioramas you'd make for elementary school projects.

The movie came to a rapid conclusion after Vernon's/Astaire's demise, even though Irene lived on and had a pretty interesting second act -- briefly continuing her showbiz career, remarrying several times and eventually becoming an animal rights activist -- until her death at age 75 in 1969. The Hollywood version of their lives skipped over lots of other interesting tidbits -- the Castles toured with an all-black orchestra, their long-time personal assistant (played in the movie by the inestimable, and very white, Walter Brennan) was also a black man, and their manager (the "entrepreneuse" mentioned earlier) was reportedly a lesbian – although the movie hinted at this since the character met the Castles while she was travelling through Europe with a female companion. Of course, two women can travel though Europe and share a hotel room and that doesn't necessarily mean they are gay. Whereas if two dudes were to do that, the odds change dramatically. In fact, that story was made into a movie a few years ago: *J. Edgar*.

The Castles' story strikes me as a film begging for a modern-day remake, a la *Moulin Rouge!* as directed by Baz Luhmann. Their lives contain so many elements of dramatic and societal significance: the nature of fame, the impact of war, issues involving race, class distinctions and sexual identity, animal rights -- all wrapped up in romance and with plenty of opportunities for big production numbers where populations of entire cities break out in vigorous walking. And when the scene is recreated -- where the entrepreneuse first meets the dancing couple -- she can stand tall and proudly proclaim her modern-day identity:" I... AM... A... MOMAGER!"

Oh, sorry -- that dialogue is from another script under development: *The Story of the Kardashian Clan -- Episode 1: What a Bunch of Entrepre-losers*.

Cat-Shit Crazy

One summer day when I was eleven I was playing football in the backyard with a friend and turned awkwardly to catch a pass, rolling painfully over on my left ankle. I came inside, sniffling a bit -- my mother asked what was wrong and when I told her, she said I'd probably just sprained my ankle and it would feel better in a day.

That night I couldn't sleep from the discomfort. When I got out of bed the next morning I limped into the kitchen for breakfast. My mother asked what was wrong and I said, "My foot REALLY hurts..." She told me to "stop faking." When I insisted I was in real pain, she took a look and my foot was swollen about twice its normal size. Now we went to the emergency room (in a hospital where my mother was employed as a social worker), where I had an x-ray which showed a hairline fracture of a bone in my foot. I got it wrapped and they gave me crutches to use for a few days. My mother knew the doctor who examined me and when he said my foot was broken, I looked at my mother and said, "I told you so!" My mother turned toward the doctor and said, laughing, "I told him he was faking!" They both thought this was very amusing and I failed to understand how my deep, distressing pain could be the source of adult amusement.

Good thing our cats can't talk...

After we moved up to the lake house, my wife decided to take on the primary responsibility for cat care. This was no cavalier decision; as you may recall, we've got five of the buggers living with us and each one gives us paws... er, pause to reconsider why we ever decided to become "crazy cat people" in the first place.

Anyway, I have suddenly been absolved of responsibility for a variety of tasks that took up a fair amount of my time each day -- supplying food and drink, combing through litter boxes, and most significantly the elbow grease required for puke-stain removal. I don't think any of our cats leave "deposits" more than the average cat does, but when you annualize those singular occurrences and multiply them times five, barely a ~~week day~~ hour went by that I wasn't huddled over a hardwood floor/carpet/couch/bedspread without a damp paper towel and bottles of Carbona and Febreze in hand(s).

When Carol told me she felt I'd been saddled with the responsibility long enough and she was going to take it on, I first thanked her and then asked if she was embracing this task out of a tremendous sense of guilt due to some deep, dark secret she was keeping from me. She paused and thought for a moment and then assured me that wasn't the case. Of course, now that this was Carol's project, it was going to handled Carol's way. This meant:

- Carol made her own litter boxes (out of large storage bins -- based on a recommendation she read on the internet).

- We were now using a new, plant-based litter (commercially available, but can be cheaply substituted for by purchasing a markedly-similar brand of animal feed at a farm supply store -- based on a recommendation she read on the internet).

- She was reconsidering whether the cats were eating the "right kind of food." When I pointed out that we'd managed to maintain the oldest members of our current brood in good health for the last 13 years and the eldest of our two original cats to age 20 on the same cuisine, she told me she would discuss diet with the veterinarian -- having read some recommendations on the internet.

- Rather than taking our grand-cat Miles (he is our son's cat but we've had legal custody of him for the last 5 years), who is the one long-hair in our coven and requires the occasional "lion cut," to a professional groomer, she purchased an electric pet-hair clipper and decided to handle the trim herself. She felt confident in her ability to do this after watching the vet buzz one quick swipe off Miles's butt and then followed it up by viewing a number of YouTube cat-clipping videos on the internet. She bought the clipper from Amazon.com, which I understand is also on the internet.

But please don't think I'm trying to sound ungrateful, or I'm second-guessing any of Carol's decisions. She felt if we were more vigilant in our grooming practices, the cats would ingest less hair and therefore produce less hairballs. That made sense. She felt if they were fed more easily-digested food, they would produce less waste product (both fore and aft). That also made sense. She felt if we took a more holistic approach to cat ownership, it would result in a happier household for all of us. That made no fucking sense at all.

To wit -- the feline-focused lifestyle was almost immediately put to the test when our cat Chloe developed a case of explosive diarrhea. I'm talking nuclear here; it was like a fire hose of liquid cat shit being sprayed on any previously dry and not-a-litter-box surface.

Now, a brief aside about this particular cat: Chloe was a stray who showed up at our door (along with her sister Sophie) 13 years ago. We coaxed the two of them inside, which took a few days, and once we did they were promptly transported to the vet for shots and spaying. Chloe, we quickly discovered, was a sociopath. Other than those occasions where we've had to chase her around the house to get her in a carrier for some reason, we have literally not put a hand on her -- because she won't let us. She gets along fine with the other cats, and is absolutely devoted to her sister, but she'll have nothing to do with human beings whatsoever. If you've ever been to visit us and have seen the cats, you've never laid eyes on this one. Sophie was also initially quite skittish and didn't like to be handled, but over the years she decided we posed no threat and became a very affectionate kitty who happily cuddles next to us on the couch or bed and enjoys being petted and brushed. Chloe, on the other hand, will be stretched out in front of an open door, laying in the warming sunshine, eyes closed and purring contentedly -- and then if one of us approaches her general vicinity, her eyes pop open and ZWING! she flies out of the room. My point here is that if any of the other cats had been afflicted with the runs, our affection for them would lead to grave concern and a relentless pursuit for a cure so they could be returned to their prior healthy and loving state. But Chloe -- not quite as much.

Anyway -- Chloe had apparently been suffering this malady for a few weeks, but we never saw which of the cats was leaving the trail of slurry behind them. Once we moved up to the lake, we finally caught Chloe mid-spray one evening (you know when you were a kid and your dad was watering the lawn, and you'd be inside behind a window and he'd spray the hose at you full-force and it made that pounding sound against the side of the house? That's what Chloe's affliction sounded like.) and promptly made an appointment to have her checked out.

The vet was a charming woman and quite thorough and obviously a "cat person." Chloe was hyperventilating through the entire exam but stayed still and didn't hiss or sink her teeth or claws into the vet (which she's done to both of us in the past. And by "the past," I mean in the fifteen minutes before leaving the house when we had to catch her to get her in the carrier.). The vet made some observations and recommended blood work and x-rays as long as we already had Chloe in the office. Sure, sure - it's only money, right? We wanted a conclusive diagnosis, regardless of treatment options. We left with a traumatized cat, a vial of antibiotics, and a bill for $300.

The vet called the next day with results of the tests -- of course, they were all IN-conclusive. It could be this, or that, or that, or that or possibly that... I think she laid out the diagnoses in order from least- to most-expensive to treat. At some point, the words "biopsy" and "exploratory surgery" were introduced into the conversation and Carol clearly stated, "We are NOT interested in anything invasive." They agreed on next steps and we were now ordering a probiotic dietary supplement (I think John Stamos endorses it) to help counter the effects of the antibiotic. And maybe we would consider a course of steroids. A few minutes later the vet called back to say, "Oh, and I don't think I mentioned before -- it could also be THIS..." which I believe would require the most costly course of treatment of all, combining surgery, chemo, prescription diet, aromatherapy and recovery time at a clinic in Baden-Baden. We reiterated our preference for starting with small steps.

Anyway, Chloe is several days into the moderate course of treatment and while she's still crapping up a storm, at least she's doing it within the confines of the storage bin cat boxes (each is big enough to hold the entire transcript of the O.J. Simpson trial). She seems a touch less jumpy around us; perhaps she now realizes just how much we care about her well-being and some of her icy reserve is beginning to melt. Or maybe she's just zonked from the pills. Through it all -- Carol has taken the lead in pill-administering, litter-cleaning, poop-pickup and carpet shampooing. The other day I wanted to express how much I admired her dedication during this crisis and so walked over to offer some affectionate words of encouragement and a loving caress. She saw me coming and ZWING! she flew out of the room.

I wonder if what Chloe has is contagious? I hope not, since we've already ruled out anything invasive.

Quote Vadis

As part of an employment search, I spent a lot of time on LinkedIn. It's not much help in finding a job -- but it's an awesome resource for the blog.

"People often say that motivation doesn't last. Well, neither does bathing. That's why we recommend it daily." -- Zig Ziglar

> Those who ignore the bathing recommendation will be seated in the Engineering section.

"It costs $0.00 to be a decent human being." -- Unknown

> Did you catch that, Donald Trump?

"It doesn't make sense to hire smart people and then tell them what to do; we hire smart people so they can tell us what to do." -- Steve Jobs

> And yet my requests for mo' money go unheeded.

"Leaders who don't listen will eventually be surrounded by people who have nothing to say." -- Andy Staley

> Leaders who have nothing to say will eventually be surrounded by reporters when they announce their entry into politics.

"If you tell the truth you don't have to remember anything." -- Mark Twain

> I didn't have a brain fart; I was just being "truthful."

"If serving someone is beneath you, then leadership is above you." -- Unknown

> And yet our CEO sends an admin out to fetch his coffee.

"Do not tolerate brilliant jerks. The cost to teamwork is too high." -- Reed Hastings

> Do like most companies do – promote them into "Internal Consultant" positions.

"Without data you're just another person with an opinion." -- W. Edwards Deming

> So <u>you</u> say.

"Any success that happens at the expense of your health, your family or your character is not real success." -- Unknown

> Well, I already sacrificed my character to get this job in the first place, so we're really just down to the first two.

"At the end of the day it's not about what you have or even what you've accomplished... It's about who you've lifted up, who you've made better. It's about what you've given back." -- Denzel Washington

> My calendar is swamped; can we try for next week?

"Getting the right people in the right jobs is a lot more important than developing a strategy." -- Jack Welch

> Uh, people who are willing to work for a company without a strategy are the "wrong" people by default.

"The sidelines are not where you want to live your life. The world needs you in the arena." -- Tim Cook

> Isn't the arena where they release the lions who then maul you to death?

Blue Genius

I usually come up with something clever in these emails to introduce my latest blog post, but in this case I've put all the creativity into the post and really don't have anything left over to share with you here.

I'm exhausted.

Well, they've just announced the 2015 MacArthur Fellows -- i.e., the "genius grants" -- and again my name is nowhere to be found on the list. I checked, twice. Honestly, I'm not sure how much longer I can sustain this level of brilliance without the appropriate recognition. Inspiration is fleeting.

This year's honorees each receive a stipend of $625,000, payable in quarterly installments over 5 years. While I'm not quite sure what a "stipend" is, my disappointment isn't all about the money. Yes, it's largely about the money but there's also the component of being acknowledged for what I've done creatively and what I could do in the future with $625K burning a hole in my pocket. The foundation website mentions the award permits recipients "the flexibility to pursue their own artistic, intellectual, and professional activities in the absence of specific obligations or reporting requirements." That is really a perfect set-up for me at the moment -- I've just been laid off from my job after 7+ years with the company and am completely without specific obligations. There are some reporting requirements, but those are at the behest of the Department of Unemployment Insurance. Once the grant payments start rolling in, I'll set aside being on the dole and can always reopen my claim once the stipend runs out.

"Stipend" -- it seems to be built around the word "spend," so maybe it has something to do with how I'm required to distribute the money to support the local economy? I'm just spit-balling here -- once I see the cash deposited in my account, I'll allocate some of my intellectual activity into further researching the meaning.

Again this year the recipients come from a wide variety of backgrounds -- scientists, community activists, artists. Well, they seem to cast a pretty broad net for "artists:" I see a tap dancer and a puppeteer among the winners. I bet right now the puppeteer is berating himself for not tap dancing while dangling his marionettes, thinking he could have doubled his award. Another of the winners is a playwright. Now, this inspires me: I'm going to write a play about my quest to be nominated for a MacArthur grant. ~~If~~ When I win, that'll be so meta.

Maybe "stipend" is another word for a wire transfer? Or cashier's check? I hope the money comes soon so I can start to really dig into this.

There is a poet in this year's group, and part of why she was honored was because, in her latest work, she "abandons all punctuation." That seems like a pretty low bar that I could easily meet if not exceed with minimal effort dedication to my craft and without working up much of a sweat its good to have an aspirational goal still within reach

Well, as Shakespeare (who never won a genius grant, and his grasp of punctuation was pretty shaky) wrote: "What's past is prologue." While I'm not sure what that means, either, cutting and pasting it here has led to a moment of even greater creative inspiration: tap-dancing marionettes performing *The Tempest*. I just need to stage it in a suitably gritty, contemporary setting while working the themes of climate change and displaced peoples into the production. Sounds like a sure-fire 2016 winner to me!

I'll need a little help getting this underway so one of the anonymous MacArthur people can see my brilliant creativity in person. If you'd like to stipend me (am I saying that correctly?) I promise to reimburse you right after I'm featured in next year's announcement, especially since with this approach I'm likely to at least triple, if not quadruple, the usual payout. Talk about genius...

Exhaust-ing Weekend

Today's painting tip: work from wet to dry. This means you should drink heavily before starting and keep painting until you sober up.

[I'll get off the lake house updates soon enough – although perhaps not soon enough for you, dear reader.]

This past weekend we made an impromptu trip up to Maine since my wife's oldest brother Emmett (who, in an amazing coincidence, is also my oldest brother-in-law) and his wife Kathleen had some time off and wanted to come see the new house and help out with any remaining projects. Hmm… yes, we could think of a few small tasks with which they could assist...

We already had plans to attend a concert on Friday night (Todd Rundgren, and if you say "Todd WHO?" then please just stop reading this blog or having anything to do with me at all), so once the show was over we hopped in the car and got on our way. We were on the road starting around 10:30pm and made it to the house around 1:15am. It was a wonderful drive, except for the: a) surprising amount of traffic, b) blinding band of rainstorms, c) exhaustion, d) brightly glowing "LOW TIRE PRESSURE WARNING! BLOWOUT IMMINENT! GET OUT OF THE CAR AND WALK!" warning light that came on about 30 miles into the drive (which, of course, we ignored) and e) heavy fog that descended upon us just as we got off the Maine Turnpike and onto the back roads. We experienced the entire range of foggishness – "light mist," "slight squint required," "hazy recollection," "where the fuck is the road?" Despite the obscured view, we managed to make it to the house unscathed.

Since we didn't get into bed until close to 2am, I slept in the next morning until nearly 6:30. I then drove to the nearest gas station to check the tire pressure, and the passenger-side front tire was as underinflated as a balloon animal assembled by a clown with emphysema. [If that turn of phrase didn't amuse you, feel free to insert your choice of breast or penis metaphor here.] The obvious choice would have been to put the spare on, but considering that would have made us (homonym alert!) four-for-four re: different tires on each corner of the car, I decided to have a complete new set installed --

peace of mind for the many trips we're planning to make up north in the months to come.

One hour and $550 dollars later, I left with a new set of wheels filled with nitrogen. Why nitrogen? Apparently, it's an inert gas and therefore superior to the normal "air" used to inflate tires. While any experience I've had with gas could hardly be labeled as "inert," I decided it was preferable to the usual inflationary process because, and this is very important, the shop didn't charge me anything extra for it. The only drawback from this decision was my fault – I'm no chemist, so I confused nitrogen with helium and thought it would be fun to suck some of the gas out from the tire through the valve. However, rather than amusing myself and others by speaking in a high, squeaky voice I instead experienced "the bends."

Coming back from the tire expedition, I found Emmett and Kathleen at the house. Their six-hour drive from Westchester County had taken a mere nine hours spread over two days due to massive traffic fleeing from New York State on Friday afternoon. They were very complimentary about the new place and despite the exhausting trip still seemed eager to assist with the list of projects for which we sought their help. Before getting underway, I offered coffee and all said yes. Two hours later I had masterfully brewed two out of three cups of java due to my meticulous process and because I kept knocking over one of the mugs. I pride myself on my coffee-brewing technique, using only single-cup pour-over unbleached filters filled with Indonesian coffee beans shit by civet cats, harvested by teenage virgins, roasted by members of the Friars Club, crushed by defeat, and transported to this country using technologies not yet invented to maintain freshness. Em and Kathleen were so impressed with my brew that they insisted that I get them coffee from Cumberland Farms for the remainder of their stay.

I forget what we accomplished Saturday afternoon because there was a lot of beer involved.

Sunday morning I slept in until 6:45; it's nothing but lazy mornings for me at the lake! After returning from Cumberland Farms with inferior coffee for certain fusspots, we decided the first task for the day would be to paint the living/dining room. The existing color was a blue-green that could only be described as "Southwest Algae:" we'd instead selected a color called "Cream Puff" because we were hungry at the time we bought the paint. Emmett took command and assured us with a crew of four we'd knock out the job in an hour. I asked how long it would take with a crew of three since I hate to paint – hate it hate it hate it. I did, however, tape off much of the trim since I wanted to be a "team player." Using duct tape was perhaps not my best choice for the task. While those three painted, I cut the grass and reduced the number of rocks I ran over this time to a mere seven.

The painting took more time than estimated, but only by a factor of six. Once done the rooms looked fantastic. Regrettably, the longer-than-expected painting effort meant we hadn't gotten to the other tasks for which Emmett's expertise was required. He and Kathleen graciously agreed to stay an extra day to help out. I was more than happy to ditch work on Monday; regrettably, Carol had to return home that night since she had a full patient load the next day. We cleaned up from our respective chores and headed out for dinner at a favorite spot that put Carol close to the highway for her drive back to Boston. After our meal, Carol headed home and the three of us went back to the lake.

I forget what we accomplished Sunday evening because there was a lot of Irish Mist and Maker's Mark involved.

Monday morning and you already know the routine – off to Cumberland Farms for three big coffees (do the math) and then it was time to install a new bathroom exhaust fan. I'd removed the existing fan for a variety of reasons; foremost among them was that the previous owner had dealt with an annoying rattle by sticking a Q-tip into the inner workings, and also that the fan was a literal vortex, sucking up cigarette smoke -- the entire workings were covered with a layer of nicotine so thick that any further description offered here would be beyond disgusting. After removing the old fan I'd covered up the hole in the ceiling by stapling a piece of cardboard across it. When Emmett pulled down the improvised cover to take a look at the opening, he was quickly covered by a blizzard of insulation that came spilling out from the rafters. He was not amused.

After wrestling with the new fixture, we (meaning Emmett) were "thisclose" to completing the installation, needing only to connect the wiring. While I shouldn't have been surprised, considering how smoothly all the other house projects have gone, we discovered the cable was about six inches too short to allow it to be connected to the wiring in the fan. Time for a trip to the hardware store (Trip #147 in the two months since we closed on the house). "And bring back more coffee!" Kathleen requested. We jumped in Emmett's van and zipped over to pick up the additional wire and the coffees. If only we'd remembered to bring our wallets with us. I drove back to the house to retrieve them and returned to the hardware store. I looked for Emmett in the electrical aisle – not there. I realized that the next most logical place to find him would be at the other end of the store – the gun counter. Y'see, in Maine they sell guns and ammo pretty much everywhere. Emmett was deep in conversation with the clerk about the array of guns, shotguns and rifles (to my untrained, pacifist eyes it appeared they carried every model of handgun known to man). Emmett pointed out the sniper's rifle on display... now, if you were a sniper wouldn't you be issued a rifle at the time of certification? And if you lost or misplaced yours, would you go to Ace Hardware for a replacement? Emmett bought some ammunition he said was unavailable to him back home in NY (he is a responsible gun-owner, as much as it pains my pacifist, gun-fearing heart to utter such a phrase) – special bullets that would explode upon impact with their target. In the interest of public safety, I should include Emmett's address here in case you are a criminal and were thinking of staging a home invasion at his place – I will strongly discourage you from doing so, especially after his most recent purchase. I mentioned to Emmett that, during Trip #103, I'd seen an elderly couple (in their 80s) buying $300 worth of ammo. The husband looked to be the older and more frail of the two; the wife pulled out her credit card to pay for the purchase, and when she went to sign the sales slip her hand shook so much that I wanted to put a maraca in it and sign up for tango lessons. I would also strongly advise that you not plan to invade this couple's home, since there is no way in HELL to predict where their shots might be aimed. I would in fact just flat out advise against even walking down their street.

We came home with the wire and finished up the installation. Fan and light worked like a charm – success! Estimated time to install: one hour. Actual time to install: six weeks (from when I'd removed the old fixture) and three hours (2:45 to put it up and 0:15 to buy coffee).

While we were struggling with this task, Kathleen calmly and efficiently managed to: trim a hedge, assemble a table, sort the recycling and knit an afghan – all while texting with her two daughters practically non-stop to thwart any attempts to burn down the house in their parents' absence.

Final project – put the dock in the water. The house came with a two-piece rolling dock, only one section of which actually has wheels on it. That was easily placed in the lake. The other section is just a big ol' slab of aluminum. You know how light aluminum is – think foil, or beer cans. This section of dock must have weighed 300 pounds. Emmett can dead-lift 305 pounds (coincidentally, if I tried to lift 305 pounds I'd also be dead), but it was still quite a struggle to get the section up off the ground and align it with the wheeled section. Ninety minutes and two fingers (mine) later, we had the dock assembled. Monday was a spectacular day – bright blue skies, temperature in the low 80s, the whole lake spread out in front of us – so of course we loaded up the van and hit the road. I needed to get back to Boston and didn't want to get caught up in rush-hour traffic, and Emmett and Kathleen planned to continue on to Lake George to meet up with friends and field more frantic texts from their daughters regarding other imminent household disasters.

All in all, a very productive weekend and Carol and I are quite indebted to E & K for all their help. Of course, as tirelessly as we worked, with limited time available, it was inevitable that there would be a little friction among us on occasion. Emmett implemented a very effective way to deal with any vitriol directed his way – he'd shake that box of ammo and immediately the disturbance was quelled. Carol and I had a few tense moments between us but got past them quickly. At times like this, I remember the old adage re: "Count to ten before you respond to anything in anger." That's good advice, although after installing the dock I hope it will be just as effective if I can only count to eight.

Cliché-WHAT?

A fool and his money are soon parted. Hey, where's my wallet?

You only hurt the one you love. However, the one you love paid you back by sleeping with all your friends.

A spoon full of sugar helps the medicine go down. Kind of ironic if you're diabetic.

A friend in need is a friend best avoided.

Beauty is in the eye of the beholder. Are those new glasses?

There's no such thing as a free lunch. There's always a meeting afterward.

Never put off until tomorrow what you can badger someone else to do for you today.

Actions speak louder than words. Profanity amps it up a bit, though.

Any friend of yours is a friend of mine. I hate you.

If at first you don't succeed, there's always another election cycle.

You can't teach an old dog new tricks. You can't teach a cat anything.

Good things come to those who wait. Better things come to those who shop online.

He's cool as a cucumber and twice as seedy.

Birds of a feather flock together, so flock you.

It was a labor of love, but the breakup was effortless.

There's more than one way to skin a cat, but don't let PETA know.

He's the salt of the earth, but I'm on a low-sodium diet.

If the shoe fits, wear it. If it doesn't, wear it to a wedding.

Possession is 9/10ths of the law, as long as you're holding less than an ounce.

It was like shooting fish in a barrel – there was water everywhere.

The early bird catches the worm. That's why I sleep in.

Time flies when you're having fun. How long have you been grounded?

Let sleeping dogs lie. You can get the truth out of them once they wake up.

There's no time like the present. Thank God it's happy hour.

Many hands make light work. Hey, where's my wallet?

Aphorism Schism

Idle hands are the devil's playground. Here's something I just typed up.

A bird in the hand means I'll not be exchanging high-fives with you any time soon.

Keep your friends close and your enemies can eliminate all of you at once.

Those who don't learn from history are doomed to repeat the tenth grade.

Three things can not be long hidden: the sun, the moon, and that stain on the carpet.

It is better to light a single candle than to curse the darkness. But who can find a candle when you bang your shin on the way to the bathroom in the middle of the night?

The definition of insanity is doing the same thing over and over again and you put something in my coffee, didn't you?

A journey of a thousand miles begins with a dead cellphone.

Two roads diverged in a wood, and I took the one less traveled by, and I got so fucking lost.

It does not matter how slowly you go as long as you're not in front of me on the expressway.

By believing passionately in something that does not yet exist, we keep those online dating services in business.

Fortune favors the brave. I guess that's why I fear trying to balance my checkbook.

A man's reach should exceed his grasp, or what's a step-ladder for?

Some see things as they are and ask, "Why?" I dream things that never were and ask, "Does Ambien have the same effect on you?"

Chance favors the prepared mind. What just happened?

Many people die at twenty-five and aren't buried until they're seventy-five. No wonder it's been so quiet around here.

It's not what you start in life, it's what you finish. Like that time wh

Many men go fishing their entire lives not knowing it is not fish they are after. Instead, they should have been on the lookout for double-negatives.

A chain is only as strong as its weakest link. That's why Circuit City went out of business.

There is only one way to avoid criticism: do nothing, say nothing, and be nothing. OK, I guess there are three ways to avoid criticism.

What we see depends on what we look for. I'm looking for trouble, and right now I see you.

I try. I fail. I try again. The day is shot.

We are what we imagine ourselves to be. What we really are is just too damn depressing to contemplate.

Blow Me

There's an opportunity to hear a "harp" before ascending into Heaven...

I recently had another birthday and again wasn't gifted with what I really wanted -- an harmonica.

I've been hinting at wanting one for many years, having offered subtle hints and suggestions along the lines of:

- "Wow! Did you hear that guy wailing on an harmonica? Sure wish I had one so I could learn to play."

- "Honey, do you know anyone who plays an harmonica? No? Well, I know what would change that..."

- "What would I like for my birthday? Gee, I'd really love an harmonica."

Now, please don't think I'm one of those "make a fuss over me because it's My Special Day" sort of people -- I'm not, I'm really not. Quite frankly, I'd be happiest if there were no acknowledgement whatsoever regarding the occasion. Birthdays are an odd celebration to begin with, since the accomplishment they are recognizing is that you managed not to die during the previous year. It's an anniversary, but not like a wedding anniversary -- a wedding anniversary is supposed to commemorate that one or the other of you managed to attract a mate and, despite your in-laws' efforts to the contrary, continue to live together and possibly even share a joint checking account. There's some effort involved. It's something you choose to do. The "event" that perhaps merits celebration regarding our births should be the anniversary of the date when our parents decided to engage in the act of sexual congress that later resulted in our slippery entrance into the world. For many of you, your parents were so enamored of each other that their passion resulted in you being born just nine months after they married. Or, in my case, being born just six months after.

A birthday is different - none of us choose to be born, much less on a specific date. A birthday just means you managed to plod through another 12 months of dreary existence on this earth while avoiding being sneezed upon and contracting swine flu, or run over by a bus, or "accidentally" mixing prescription drugs and cinnamon schnapps. What little effort may have been expended in these avoidance maneuvers is minimal at most. So, cheerful sort that I am, I'm happy for my birthday to be just another ordinary day of avoiding sneezes and buses. But -- if my wife or son ask, "What do you want for your birthday?" and I offer a gentle and unobtrusive suggestion such as "I'd like some warm socks" or "I'd enjoy going out for a hamburger" or, most significantly, "I'D LIKE AN HARMONICA," then dammit! they'd better gimme those socks/that burger/AN HARMONICA.

Actual conversation, reproduced verbatim and occurs every year:

- WIFE: "What kind of birthday cake would you like?"

- ME: "I'd like a JELL-O cake."

- WIFE: "I am not making you a JELL-O cake."

She says a JELL-O cake is "gross." Well, I think potato salad is "gross" but I don't tell her she can't eat it, especially if she asked for it for her birthday (although I would not allow her to eat it anywhere within a thousand-yard proximity to me). Why doesn't she just tell me what kind of cake *she* would enjoy for my birthday? And then ask me to go to the store and pick one up?

See, this is exactly the kind of fracas I want to avoid by side-stepping the societal obligation to "celebrate" my birthday. It creates tension, angst, dissent, tumult... all feelings that leave me feeling rather blue. And what instrument best captures the essence of the blues? AN HARMONICA.

Am I the only one who sees the irony here? The one gift in the whole world that would make me happiest is precisely what I need to express my despair. Receiving an harmonica would fill me with such joy that I'd no longer have any need to play it.

Perhaps what I should get for my birthday is an oxymoron. Especially since I'm now starting to feel like one.

Inexhorrible

I literally had to do the math to recall how old I turn today. That's a bummer.

(BTW: Not fishing for birthday wishes -- but will accept your checks and gift cards.)

Another birthday is here, so let's assess how I've done with my goals since the last one:

- Get in shape: That shape is "rotund."

- Read more: The disclaimers that come with my prescriptions go on for pages.

- Make new friends: First step was to alienate most of my old ones.

- Travel: Some nights I make as many as three trips to the bathroom.

- Learn a new language: I now know how to say "mofo" in Armenian.

- Find something to be thankful for every day: On those mornings when I step into my slippers and don't discover a hairball in them, I am thankful.

- Love more: Carol is curious where I go on the weekends.

- Watch less TV: Thank God for streaming services.

- Get closer to the earth: I've slipped and fallen to the ground several times.

- Worry less: I'm concerned I haven't made enough progress with this one.

- Speak truth to power: Stop letting authority figures intimidate me, so I use my cellphone in the library.

- Embrace failure: Actually, I found this one on Carol's list. No wonder she's been hugging me so much lately.

Years ago I worked at a company where the director was fond of saying, "Every day I can wake up and put both feet on the ground is a good day." His words inspired me to set my expectations at an absolute minimum.

Oui, Je Regrette Tout

People often say they "share" their birthday with certain celebrities or others of note. I don't share my birthday with anyone.

It's my birthday today, a time for reflection and early-in-the-day drinking.

It's pretty safe to say I'm well past the halfway point in my life, barring advances in cryogenics or any more broken mirrors. The road behind is longer than the road ahead, and I'm running out of change for the tolls. Regrets, I've had a few, but then again who's counting?

Here are a few things I would have done differently, if I could turn back time and get Cher's voice out of my head. Hope you can learn from my mistakes.

- Never give a Snuggie or a Chia Pet as a gift to a loved one.

- Eat at your own risk in a "kosher-style" deli. "-style" means "not quite."

- Put your family first. That way you can hide behind them when the going gets tough.

- Learn to speak another language, if for no other reason than the curse words are usually awesome.

- Prejudice based on race, creed, color, or sexual orientation is always wrong. However, discrimination based on wardrobe or personal hygiene is completely justified.

- Love is the answer, but I forget what the question was.

- Drive for show, putt for dough, try not to take the sand wedge out of your bag.

- You never have a second chance to make a first impression, so let the expletives fly.

- Eat dessert first. That way you fill up quickly and save money on the tip.

- Professional athletes and celebrities aren't "heroes" - the real heroes are found in comic books.

- Respect your elders -- they have wisdom to share and control your inheritance.

- Practice random acts of kindness. Revenge takes careful planning.

- If you're married, or living with a significant other -- never go to bed mad. That's what couches are for.

- Live every day like it's your last, and you'll never need to change your passwords.

- "Love" and "sex" are not the same thing, but you'll have fun trying to sort through the confusion.

- Sow your oats while you're young. Interestingly, as you get older you'll still be relying on fiber to get you through the day.

It all comes down to the Golden Rule, found in so many religious and social traditions: "Do unto others as you would have them do unto you." This is the best thing you can live by, unless your neighbor is a dentist or plumber.

Marriage Wows

We're spending the week at the beach with friends who are on their honeymoon. We're serving not so much as "chaperones" as "advisors." They don't seem to be heeding any of the advice we've offered...

We've just attended the wedding of our closest friends -- my best friend Bert married my wife's best friend Marsha. We introduced them 11 years ago and their passion for one another ignited like wet cardboard. However, a couple of years back they were again in the same place at the same time in our company (as much as we'd like to believe that last factor was essential, it probably wasn't); drier conditions prevailed and FWOOSH! their situation suddenly became combustible.

The wedding was beautiful -- a perfect late-summer day; the ceremony staged outdoors at a charming cottage in downtown Greenville, South Carolina overlooking a lovely park; a small audience of family and dear friends; an excellent meal, and to cap it off the DJ played the most profound of all disco songs -- Kool and the Gang's "Get Down On It," which features this chorus:

"Get down on it, get down on it, get down on it, get down on it,

Get down on it, get down on it, get down on it, get down on it!"

Whenever I hear this song, I picture Kool hunched over a legal pad, pencil in hand, with half-empty cans of Diet Coke and smoldering cigarettes and beer bottles strewn about the recording studio. Kool looks tired and disheveled, and barely notices when the rest of the Gang walks in. "Whuzzup, K?" one Gang-member asks. "Did you finish that dope tune you were working on yesterday?" "Naw, man. I'm stuck... can't come up with a last line for it." "Read us what you've got so far and maybe all of us working together can bring on the funk." "Sure, sure," Kool replies, and proceeds to recite the seven lines he's scribbled so far. ."..... and that's where I'm lost, fellahs." The rest of the Gang start to think out loud, one tapping on piano keys, another absent-mindedly strumming a guitar, a third looking into space. Several suggestions are offered but quickly dismissed as being "too wordy," "doesn't flow," or "changes the narrative point of view." But after a while one Gang-ster (which one is lost to history, and the ensuing court battles over authorship and publishing rights eventually break up the band. But at this very moment their collective creative quest still unites them in musical brotherhood) looks up and says, "Hey, what about..." and the now-completed song goes on to assume its place in dance floor history.

Our friends expressly prohibited the d.j. (who goes by the name "DJ Skid" -- can you tell he's a white guy?) from playing any of the group-dance songs that one normally hears at a wedding -- *Y.M.C.A.*, the Electric Slide, others of that ilk. They're our age, second marriage for both, and those kinds of tunes just didn't fit into the tenor of the event. But when *Born to Run* came on, the groom leapt onto the dance floor, resplendent in his Brooks Brothers suit, and began to thrash with abandon. His choreography mimicked that of the two "wild and crazy guys" of SNL fame, with all the finger-pointing, heel-wiggling, and hip-gyrating they displayed while walking to answer the door when they thought "American foxes" had rung the bell.

Going to a wedding inevitably leads to comparisons with other weddings you've attended (and of course your own). While Bert and Marsha organized an elegant and tasteful affair, it spurred thoughts of other nuptials we've been to that were somewhat less impressive:

- An open bar every other hour.

- A polka band attempting *Black Magic Woman*, with a trumpet taking the lead guitar part.

- A rabbi who paused mid-ceremony and yelled at the photographer to stop taking pictures.

- A reception where the groom's father engaged in "dirty dancing" with his son's new wife.

- Another reception where the dessert was JELL-O.

We've been invited to the wedding but not the reception; the reception but not the wedding; "provisionally" to the wedding "if enough people decline so there's room for you," and once we were invited to the same wedding twice and the groom backed out both times. The explanation the first time was "jitters;" the explanation the second time was the soap opera subplot that he'd fathered a child with another woman and was going to marry her instead. Even more tragically, the jilted bride didn't return any of the wedding presents.

We lived in the South for many years and were always amused when guests would come to a wedding wearing t-shirts and shorts. These were indoor ceremonies, in churches, and sometimes a full Catholic Mass. That always flummoxed the Southern Baptists, who were expecting a 15-minute service, some cake and punch, and to be back home in an hour. Usually they'd just leave the kids in front of the TV to save on a baby sitter. The concept of R.S.V.P. was also foreign to some of these folks, who would respond to a follow-up inquiry whether they were planning to attend with, "We'll sure try."

Carol and I had a mixed ceremony, with a priest and rabbi officiating. We had a hard time finding a rabbi who would participate, as most of them declined while still encouraging us to join their congregations after we were married. We finally found a retired rabbi who would serve jointly with a priest, but then due to schedule conflicts we needed to start the search for Jewish representation anew. Yet another rabbi declined, and when I mentioned the name of the other rabbi who would have performed the service except for the scheduling conflict, this rabbi laughed dismissively and said, "You know, he has a reputation as a 'Marrying Sam'." The whole experience contributed to my decision to renounce organized religion, largely in favor of disorganized hedonism. We ended up tweaking our schedule so the retired rebbe could step in. Bert and Marsha's minister was also retired, which got me thinking -- would you want a surgeon to come out of retirement to operate on you? "Nurse, bring me a bottle of chloroform and a container of leeches - stat!"

Anyway, we're so pleased how everything turned out for our friends and they are just radiant with happiness. As they start their new life together, another poignant Kool and the Gang lyric comes to mind; from *Fresh*:

"She's so fresh, she's so fresh, she's so fresh, she's so fresh, she's so fresh,

She's so fresh, she's so fresh, she's so fresh, she's so fresh, she's so fresh,

She's so fresh, she's so fresh, she's so fresh, she's so fresh, she's so fresh,

She's so fresh, she's so fresh, she's so fresh, she's so fresh, she's so fresh,

She's so fresh, she's so fresh, she's so fresh, she's so fresh, she's so fresh."

I couldn't have said it better myself, especially that last part.

Vodka Catatonic

Some folks are dog people, some folks are cat people. I wonder how our pets feel about us?

Our cat Chloe has, like that parrot in the fabled Monty Python sketch, "ceased to be." With a bit of an assist from her loving owners...

As you may recall from this post, our cat Chloe had been experiencing... intestinal issues. We tried a conservative approach to treatment, first with antibiotics and then, when those had no discernible effect, a course of steroids. The steroids didn't help with the diarrhea either, but Chloe's slugging percentage rose nearly 100 points in a week.

The other morning I came downstairs and showered and after I completed my toilette I exited the bathroom and noticed a... distinct odor. I was fairly certain I wasn't the source since I'd just scrubbed up, so I strode over to the cat boxes to inspect. I found, outside of the receptacles, several pools of... Nah, I'm not even going to try to describe it, delicately or otherwise. It was clear that: A) the medication wasn't helping, and B) it was only a matter of time before the cat bypassed the designated area altogether and decided to go wherever she wanted in the house, much like my great-aunt sometimes did.

Carol came downstairs as I was finishing clean-up. I apprised her of the situation and it didn't take us long to agree that Chloe's time was coming to an end. We called the vet to review and she was very understanding, offering only a mild suggestion that we perhaps would consider another round of antibiotics (to which we said "Nuh-uh"), and recognizing that the next most likely causes were really serious stuff like lymphoma or a cat with a "Jewish stomach" (as some of you may know: a miserable, incurable condition). We felt since Chloe was a cat who shied from human contact that our ability to administer any medications or manage her care would be almost impossible. Under those conditions, we felt making a quick move to prevent Chloe's further suffering was the best course of action. The vet agreed and then transferred us to the front desk to set up Chloe's "end of life" appointment for later that morning; "end of life" being a euphemism for "costly veterinary visit."

We managed to get Chloe into her carrier without too much difficulty. She wasn't happy about being confined and fortunately the vet's office was a short drive away. As soon as we walked in a staff member named Renee came out, knowing why we were there, and ushered us into an examination room so we could review the protocol.

Renee asked us to sign a form that Chloe hadn't bitten anyone in the past fifteen days. I discounted any injuries obtained from putting her in the carrier twice in the last two weeks and signed the form -- if she was rabid, she took that secret to her grave. Now the hard decision came -- credit or debit? Well, before that we needed to indicate whether we wanted to be present when the vet administered the lethal injection. I asked, "Do you mean present like in the room, or in the general vicinity?" She confirmed she meant the room, and after a bit of tearful consideration we decided not to observe. This cat derived no comfort from our proximity in all her years living under our roof, so why should we be visible in her final moments to further agitate her? We then had to decide among three options:

1.   Bring her home intact to bury her.

2.   Have her cremated and have the cremains returned to us.

3.   Have her cremated with nothing given back.

Carol and I actually had talked about this before heading over. We've had cats for years and this wasn't the first "end of life" pet situation in which we'd found ourselves. When we had Felix whacked... I mean our first cat who peacefully slipped the surly bonds of Earth came home in a "cadaver bag" which we then put in a shoe box to bury in the backyard. Josh and I picked a quiet spot underneath a corner pine tree and dug a hole. We plunged the shovel into the ground three or four times and then Carol called to us from inside the house: "Hey, what happened to the TV?" (We all grieve in our own way.) We'd managed to chop the coaxial cable in two. The repair visit from Comcast cost almost as much as the vet's fees for the euthanasia. The next time we were faced with that decision, with Felix's brother Oscar (who'd reached age 20), we told the vet, "Nah - you can keep him."

So, we went with Option 3. Renee took Chloe away in the carrier and was gone only a few minutes before returning it to us, with Chloe in the hands of the vet tech who would prepare her for the injection.

We left, distressed and upset, and drove back to the house making little conversation. As we entered we were met by Sophie, the cat who had showed up along with Chloe on our doorstep all those years ago, poor little kitties abandoned by their previous owner. Sophie gave us a look that said, "I know what you did." At least, that's how we interpreted it. Then she went over to the food dish and chomped on some kibble but kept one wary eye on us the entire time she ate.

That evening we sipped a couple of stiff drinks and looked through our collection of cat photos, reminiscing about our dear Chloe and coming to grips with our decision to end her life. I know there are some folks reading this who would advocate for trying all available treatments, and maybe if it had been one of our other cats who are, how should I say, *not mental*, we might have considered a more valiant course of action. But we're at peace with our decision and feel we intervened before Chloe really started to suffer from whatever had caused our formerly chubby tabby to lose so much weight and struggle with her normally conscientious sanitary routine. I feel if Chloe were able to communicate with us from wherever she is now, she'd look at us with those big saucer eyes and say, "WHAT HAVE YOU SONS OF BITCHES DONE TO ME? FIRST YOU HAD ME KILLED AND THEN YOU HAD MET SET ON FIRE! YOU BASTARDS... I HOPE YOU ROT IN HELL!! I'M ON FIRE! OH MY GOD... I'M ON FIRE..."

Upon reflection, perhaps I can glean some of the rationale behind her mistrust of people. Rest in peace, our Little Fat Girl...

GPS-hole

It takes two to make a relationship work, but we know it's really just *one* of us who puts the most effort into it, right?

In the car late yesterday, heading for one of the warehouse stores to stock up on some bulk supplies, after which we'll go out for dinner and then grocery shop for the week before heading home. Heading in the direction of our pre-last-summer's-move neighborhood, since we know where everything is up there but still can't find our way to the corner from our new apartment.

Car is in motion, about to enter the highway, when Carol asks if there's a branch of the store closer to where we now live. I reply if she can find it and direct us to the location, I'll go that way.

Out comes the smartphone and voilà! There's another store only half the distance away. Google Maps says "5.6 mi., 15 mins." Of course, we have *just* driven past the first exit we need to take, so I make a U-ey and head back on the other side of the road.

45 minutes, umpteen missed turns and 2 screaming matches later, we still haven't found the "closer" store. "Fuck it! I'm not going to fucking BJ's now! I don't know where the fuck I am!" I calmly state. Carol responds in a huff, "Perhaps if we pull over for a moment..." Christ Almighty! She sure knows how to push my buttons.

As we start to head back toward where we think we live, we pass a supermarket on our left. I rapidly reassess our plans and decide to mitigate any further risk by moving grocery shopping to the top of our remaining priorities for the evening. At the intersection, I expertly veer across two lanes of oncoming traffic, fly into the lot and glide to a stop in an open space, just barely crumpling the fender of the car parked facing us.

We enter the store and find ourselves in the produce section. Carol prods me: "Would you like some salad tonight?" "NO!" I tranquilly respond. "Do we need any cold cuts?" "I HAVE NO FUCKING IDEA!" "How many jalapeños do you want for the chili?" "HAVEN'T YOU EVER MADE CHILI BEFORE?" "If I make sausage and peppers this week, will you want some?" "I HATE

SAUSAGE AND PEPPERS!" "What kind of ice cream do you want?" "I DON'T... uh, Peanut Butter Cup."

After we check out and put our groceries in the car, Carol says she's happy to drive home if I prefer to navigate. "Good," I think to myself, "she recognizes her limitations." I quickly pull up the directions home and promptly point us toward the wrong exit from the parking lot. "Jesus," I think to myself, "she can't use the GPS and she can't drive, either..."

After missing several road signs since it's now dark out, we finally find ourselves on a road with which Carol is familiar and she gets us home in just a few more minutes. I bring in the groceries while Carol throws our frozen pizza in the oven, and by the time everything's put away and the cats -- who have been underfoot since the moment we walked back into the house, no doubt reacting to Carol's mood -- are fed, dinner is ready.

We sit on the couch with our slices, flipping on the TV and ready to decompress from our brief excursion gone horribly wrong. The tension between us appears to be dissipating. I don't intend to make a big deal out of this mishegas and am prepared to forgive Carol for her earlier unwarranted outbursts.

I take a bite of my pizza and burn the fucking shit out of my mouth. I can't believe Carol is still being so petty AND she's willing to have me suffer second-degree burns just so she can settle the score between us? I glare at her -- she is watching the TV, not looking at me. Oh, she is SO evil -- she doesn't even glance in my direction to see if her cunning effort has succeeded. Fuming, I take another bite of my pizza and again burn the fucking shit out of my mouth. My GOD this woman is so vindictive.

After we finish our pizza, I extract my revenge. I cheerfully offer to get ice cream for both of us and short her one scoop. Then the pièce de résistance -- I recommend we watch Woody Allen's *To Rome With Love*, telling her the star-studded cast combined with the filmmaker's pedigree ensures it will be hilarious.

Heh-heh-heh. Talk about mis-direction...

Defining Moment

This post has to do with a list of obscure words. If you don't care for it, then you can go to spell.

As deluded as I may be in considering myself a "writer," I've certainly enjoyed the challenge of putting pen to paper (or, in my case, brainwaves to Interocitor) and coming up with brief essays that others may also derive pleasure from. Or, since my grammar should be exemplary in this instance - "'... that from which others derive also may pleasure." Of course, in addition to deciding upon subject matter there's also the creative challenge of being vocabulent. Notice how I devised an adjective at the end of that last sentence to describe a hither-to undocumented state of being -- "fanciful in one's use of verbiage." I'm sure "vocabulent" will be included in a future edition of the Oxford English Dictionary, or else my next tweet.

All seriousness aside: I do occasionally come across a word I haven't encountered before or whose proper use I've misunderstood. As an example, I recently learned that "oubliette" is the French word for "omelette." Also that "toastmaster" and "sous chef" are not interchangeable. And while the best-known maxim for writers is to "write what you know," I certainly enjoy flexing my mental muscles and looking for discrete opportunities to introduce a word or phrase that, while perhaps less frequently encountered, serves to encapsulate a certain je ne sais quoi (more French, and I'm honestly not sure what it means) where everyday-wordiness simply isn't up to the task. While I realize I run the risk of leaving some of my more pedantic followers behind (because they are, literally, "walking" followers), I get a thrill when sprinkling such bon mots (yet more French! It's like I'm bi-inguinal) into my posts and knowing that at least several of my literally dozen of followers enjoy being stimulated by such intellectual crap.

I recently came across the following list of rarely encountered words, a few of which may be familiar to some of you. But for the benefit of the other somes of yous to whomse they are not yet known, I have included definitions so you won't have to scramble for a dictionary (which I, as well, did not):

- **captious:** obsessed with hats

- **bibulous:** involved in an activity which requires wearing an apron

- **tricorn:** the offspring of a unicorn and a bull

- **tenebrous:** a group of slightly less than a dozen people

- **braggadocio:** an especially pretentious Starbucks order

- **bruit:** the act of manufacturing ale or lager

- **valetudinarian:** being exceptional at parking cars

- **cenacle:** ten times as frightening as a tentacle

- **hypermnesia:** a condition where one frequently forgets how to spell words beginning with the letter "a"

- **estivation:** a guess regarding the height of a mountain

- **myrmidon:** the leader of a group of undersea nymphs involved in a criminal enterprise

- **regnant:** an apartment-dweller who breaks a lease

- **clerisy:** a priest considering conversion to Judaism

- **deracinate:** to cool down after running a marathon

- **oneiromancy:** kissing one's own reflection in a mirror

- **tatterdemalion:** what remains after running over weeds with a lawn mower

- **hypnopompic:** the state of being entranced by extravagant spectacle

- **pule:** the opposite of "pyush"

- **funambulist:** an EMT relating a humorous anecdote

Honestly, I'm not even sure my keyboard came with all the letters necessary to spell some of these. I plan to work on introducing them into my lexicon (when I can afford one -- I'm still tooling around in an aging toyoticon). BTW: wordplay involving an automobile is known as "carpaccio." And if you don't care for puns -- well, please take your beef elsewhere.

Eddy Blizzard

As I'm typing this (February 2013), we've still got a few hours to go before the snow and winds start to taper off and the historic winter storm named "Nemo" moves away from my perch in Cambridge, MA and out over the Atlantic. While final totals have yet to be established, it seems certain we'll end up with more than two feet of snow in many areas.

Two feet! That's more snow than some people see in an entire lifetime. For those of you who can't imagine what that's like, here are some analogies to help you picture it:

- Imagine a foot of snow -- and then another foot of snow on top of it. That's two feet!

- If you bought two Subway footlong subs and stacked them upright end to end, most of the fillings would immediately fall out and you'd have quite a mess on your hands. Why would you waste food like that? People are starving in Africa.

- Picture four feet of snow; two feet is half as much.

- Imagine lying on your back with your arms pointing toward the sky. I'm imagining it, and you look pretty silly.

- Try stacking the subs again but this time no onions, please.

- With snow falling at a rate as fast as 4 inches per hour, you would tire of the non-stop weather updates on TV within 20 minutes.

And let's not forget the impact of wind during this event. Winds in some sections of eastern Massachusetts and the Cape are gusting as high as 84 miles per hour. How fast and intense is an 84 mph wind gust?

- That's faster than any Yugo built could ever go, even down a steep grade with the pedal to the floor and a semi crowding your rear-view mirror.

- That's more intense than the scene in *Silence of the Lambs* where the two cops bring Dr. Lecter his extra-rare lamb chops and they end up eviscerated. I'm talking about the cops here; I don't think Lecter touches his dinner. Why would he waste food like that? People are starving in Africa.

- If you want to know what the sting of heavy, wet snow blowing into your face at 84 mph feels like -- stand in front of me and I'll slap you as hard as I can with my wet hand. Now let me do that again. OK, one more time. Oh, stop crying you big baby! You said you wanted to know what it felt like.

Well, let me turn my attention back to the TV -- they're showing the fleet of snowplows required to remove the phalanx of hyper-animated field reporters cluttering the roadways. I hope some of these analogies helped you to understand the impact of this storm and brought a simile to your face. Does it still hurt? Here, put some snow on it...

Adage Before Beauty

"He that hath knowledge spareth his words..."
Oh, the delightful irony!

When someone talking to you says "long story short," it's already too late.

Know how I play "Words With Friends?" By cursing at them.

I'm not trying to lower my cholesterol so much as quell it.

My wife was away for the weekend. At least, that's what she told me.

There but for the grace of God go I. Plus there was a *Breaking Bad* marathon on TV.

It's said, "All politics is local." That's incorrect; it should be, "All politics are insulting to the electorate."

I've begun a new exercise regimen. So far, I'm exercising my right not to follow it.

When I was a young camper I was once thrown from a horse. Now when someone asks if I'll ever saddle up again I say, "Neigh."

Avoid trying anything labelled as "new & improved" since it is likely neither.

I roasted a chicken the other night. I hope it understood my zingers were offered in jest.

Any cocktail made with more than 4 ingredients (including ice) is just not worth the effort.

What do you get when you cross a duck with a hornet's nest? You get one pretty pissed-off duck, for starters.

I fell off a ladder and through the roof. Not surprisingly, I broke out in shingles.

A man is known by the company he keeps. Please go home now.

I beat the rap on a charge of home invasion by claiming I was participating in the new "sharing economy."

An injury is sooner forgotten than an insult. That's why I kicked you, jackass.

None of us is as smart as all of us. But I is much smarter than you is.

The night has a thousand eyes. "Mississippi" runs a close second.

Quote-idian

Actually, I love motivational quotes. They often motivate me to kill the person who coined them.

"If you take care of your people your people will take care of your customers and your business will take care of itself."

That's why we're laying off all our back office staff.

"The remarkable thing is, we have a choice everyday regarding the attitude we will embrace for that day."

For the foreseeable future I'll choose to embrace a negative attitude.

"It's easier to do a job right than explain why you didn't."

But the lady at the unemployment office isn't really interested in your explanation.

"There's a way to do it better. Find it."

While you're doing that, I'll be sitting back and letting my business take care of itself.

"If everything was perfect, you would never learn and you would never grow."

Like, I just learned what the "subjunctive mood" is!

"Believe you can and you're halfway there."

Believe you can't and you can skip the trip altogether.

"Aim for the moon. If you miss, you may hit a star."

NASA vehemently disagrees.

"Don't watch the clock; do what it does. Keep going."

3:30 already? Bye -- see you tomorrow!

"A creative man is motivated by the desire to achieve, not by the desire to beat others."

> I was motivated to beat others and HR said I had to attend an anger management seminar, which I have no desire to.

"Keep your eyes on the stars and your feet on the ground."

> But maybe first move out from the middle of the sidewalk.

"It is better to fail in originality than to succeed in imitation."

> That's why, despite the publisher's urging, there was no *Moby Dick 2: Ahab's Back!*

"Success is walking from failure to failure with no loss of enthusiasm."

> But it's better to start the stroll with a fat wallet, no?

"If you can't explain it simply, you don't understand it well enough."

> For example, Trump's election.

"Only put off until tomorrow what you are willing to die having left undone."

> Guess I better put on another pot of coffee.

"A real entrepreneur is somebody who has no safety net underneath them."

> Killer idea: personal safety nets!

"The number one reason people fail in life is because they listen to their friends, family, and neighbors."

> Who does that leave to listen to, exactly?

"You've got to get up every morning with determination if you're going to go to bed with satisfaction."

> You've got to go to bed with Cialis if you're going to get it up every morning.

"Fortune sides with him who dares."

I dare whoever came alongside me and stole my fortune to give it back.

We're Not in Kansas Anymore

There are two sides to every story, but as I often tell Carol: "You got something to say -- start your OWN blog."

Carol and I were sitting on the couch the other evening, both of us reading quietly. I reached over to give her an affectionate rub on the shoulder and asked, "Do you love me?" Without looking up her immediate reply was, "What do you want?" I was stunned by her response to my sweet, gentle question and decided to ditch my follow-up query regarding her willingness to get up and bring me a bowl of ice cream.

Lately we find ourselves in the midst of a mild "failure to communicate," mostly about mundane issues but pushing us just enough off-track to lead to some occasional friction. A few weeks ago we were heading out for dinner; I was ready and cooling my heels while waiting for Carol to get dressed. "How about this?" she solicited. Since I'm familiar with her wardrobe I didn't need to look before replying, "Adorable. Let's go." She stared at me and muttered, ."".. asshole..." under her breath before heading back to her closet. I was offended by her accusation. Well, I feigned offense but that's pretty much the same response, isn't it?

I was assembling a piece of furniture and was flummoxed (as I often am) by a set of unhelpful instructions. I made a series of false starts and mis-steps, and each time as I recognized the latest snafu I exclaimed, "Oh my GOD!" in frustration. Carol kept asking if she could help me. After her sixth or seventh offer of assistance, I again replied "No" and added, "Please don't ask, 'Can I help you?' every time you hear me say in exasperation, 'Oh my GOD!'" I returned to my task, then paused and added, "Conversely -- if you hear me ask, 'Can you help me?' please don't reply with an exasperated 'Oh my GOD!'" I don't think she embraced my clarification in the spirit it was intended.

We were in the car, headed for a destination Carol was familiar with but I wasn't. Since I was behind the wheel I asked her to provide navigation. As we drove along one stretch of road, Carol said something about a sign up ahead which may have implied an imminent change in direction, but since I was passionately singing along to *Carry*

On Wayward Son on the radio I wasn't paying attention to her at that moment (a more considerate person would have provided guidance during one of the numerous instrumental interludes). She then began to shout and gesture frantically as I nearly sped past where we needed to bear left. I slammed on the brakes, spinning the wheel and fishtailing in a manner reminiscent of Steve McQueen in Bullitt. Once I'd corrected course and returned to my side of the road, I reminded her of my preference for timely directions offered in advance rather than this tumultuous last-second, arm-waving, shouting-laden approach. While I initially thought she was quietly contemplating my observation before offering an apology, I was distressed when her silence continued for the rest of our drive and in fact the remainder of the day. How ironic there was no peace when we were done with our trip.

Of course there are guidelines couples should follow to ensure effective communication. We are acquainted with them but sometimes find ourselves just not up to making the proactive effort required, falling back on bad habits and then suffering through the consequences as a result. When Carol fails to express herself appropriately, I gently admonish her and then thoughtfully point out what she should have said differently. Lately, however, Carol isn't embracing these as "teachable moments" and instead seems to feel I'm being chauvinistic and condescending toward her, while portraying myself as beyond reproach. Well, I really can't control how she chooses to respond (another guideline for effective communication between partners), so I've learned to give her the space she needs regardless of how much it wounds my soul. While it's proving to be a tiresome burden it's one I bear with minimal complaint since -- at their core -- these contretemps are transitory and insignificant and in no way interfere with our deep and abiding love for one another.

But oh my GOD if Carol doesn't bring me a bowl of ice cream one evening soon I am going to lay my weary head to rest.

Linguine Franca

Inspired by a longing for pasta, but then quickly took a right turn.

There are certain phrases that I think I know what they mean but find out later that I don't, or have misunderstood their proper usage. "Lingua franca" is one such phrase - I always thought it meant "mother tongue," but that's astray from its actual meaning of "common language." One example often given is that English is the "lingua franca" of air travel -- pilots and air traffic controllers communicate with one another in English around the world, regardless of their native language.

"Hoi polloi" is another one, although this is one phrase I understood correctly to mean "the common people." I read it is incorrect to say, "the hoi polloi," since that translates as "the the common people." It's like when you receive an invitation that says "Please R.S.V.P.;" it's redundant: "Please respond if you please." But I don't worry about the redundancy since I wasn't planning to attend anyway, open bar or not.

Not all the phrases and idioms that flummox are based in other languages - "moot point" comes to mind. It's commonly used to mean an idea rendered irrelevant due to some other action. Grammarians (and some Lutherans) argue about the meaning, with many taking the tack (or is that "tact?") the actual meaning is an idea that is debatable; one with room for discussion. However, over time the agreed-upon meaning has settled on "It's been decided so shut up, already." I used to work for a boss who always used the phrase, "It's a mute point." Believe me, I wished he would've shut up, preferably before opening his mouth.

Here are a few other phrases I've found that are commonly misused or misunderstood, or at least by me:

- **Au courant** -- contains raisins.

- **Carte blanche** -- to exceed one's credit limit; alternatively, to drive one's aunt to the store.

- **Cum laude** -- a vociferous expression of sexual pleasure.

- **De rigueur** -- a dead person; related to femme fatale; a deceased woman.

- **Ex cathedra** -- someone who no longer attends church.

- **Faux pas** -- my step-father.

- **In his cups** -- a man wearing a brassiere.

- **Je ne sais quoi** -- literally, "This is the extent of my French."

- **Mano a mano** -- man-to-man; the feminine is "Chica to Cheek.."

- **Mi casa es su casa** -- from the Spanish for "empty refrigerator."

- **Voulez vous coucher avec moi** – "I didn't realize I asked you to sleep with me; I was just singing along with the radio."

- **Persona non grata** -- someone who doesn't like hard cheeses.

- **Quid pro quo** -- from the Latin and thought to be the first tongue-twister (say it 3x fast).

- **Robbing Peter to pay Paul** -- willing to plead to a misdemeanor to avoid being convicted of a felony.

- **Shoulda, coulda, woulda** -- filled with remorse and too overwhelmed to form a complete sentence to express such a feeling.

- **Veni, vidi, vici** -- attributed to Julius Caesar, who was the first to mispronounce the phrase.

- **Zeitgeist** -- a hard cookie offered to teething babies.

While English has most of its roots in Latin, over time the language has embraced a panoply (from the Greek for playing multiple rounds of Monopoly) of expressions shanghaied from other languages. German chocolate cake, French's mustard, Swiss Miss cocoa, Spanish peanuts, and Hawaiian Punch are all examples of such influences on the vernacular. The public transportation system in Chicago is known as the El, which is Spanish for "the." Therefore, Chicagoans move around the city riding "the The." That's hard to say, so residents wrapped their mother tongues around the more easily-pronounced nickname "the El," which was in common use within the local Chicano (from the Spanish for "Chicago") community.

Speaking of Chicago -- I once attended a business meeting where the discussion centered on the particulars of a government contract with the state of Illinois. While most of the services would be offered for workers in Chicago, there was a component required for Springfield employees as well. A confused look crossed the face of one of the attendees, who asked aloud, with representatives from the state on the conference line, "Why the hell do we need to offer the service to anyone in Springfield?" I leaned over and quietly said that Springfield was the state capital of Illinois, hence... I believe, at that moment, my co-worker wished he had made a mute point.

Bitter Patter

I filed our taxes today -- if you want to read something really creative…

Looks can be deceiving. Smell, however, should be trusted implicitly.

It's not what you know, it's who the hell told you??

Pride goeth before a fall. That's why I stick to the couch.

One man's meat is another man's poison. That's why you should avoid the Beef Stroganoff at any luncheonette.

I cried because I had no shoes. Then the salesman came out with a size 10 wide and I was happy.

Give me your tired, your poor, your huddled masses yearning to breathe free, the wretched refuse of your teeming shore. No, wait -- on second thought, you can keep the wretched refuse.

If you can't stand the heat, get out of the sauna.

Who knows what evil lurks in the heart of men? Their ex-wives know.

The wages of sin is death, but they do offer a 401(k) match.

The man who has confidence in himself gains the confidence of others. At least that's what my financial advisor told me as I handed him that check.

If not us, who? If not now, when? No, next week is bad for me.

He who hesitates is lost. But he'll never ask for directions, that's for sure.

Ask me no questions and I'll tell you no lies. I guess that doesn't leave us much to talk about.

A little knowledge is a dangerous thing. I like to live dangerously.

A prophet is not recognized in his own land. Check again, I'm sure my name's on the list.

Good things come to those who wait. Yes, that's the same thing I told you yesterday.

Lightning never strikes twice in the same place, so slide over a little.

Many a true word is spoken in jest. You are stupid and ugly, LOL.

There is many a slip 'tween cup and lip, particularly after last call.

You can catch more flies with honey than vinegar, but really -- could you just close the screen door behind you?

Resolutions for the New Year

In the New Year starting on or about January 1, I hereby resolve to:

- Stop saying "Whoa!" in my Vinny Barbarino voice every time I see John Travolta on TV.

- Let those close to me know how much I love them every day, even when I'm really not feeling it.

- Play more tennis while wearing a headband, for the amusement of my opponents.

- Lose 30 pounds before my audition for the film version of *Les Miz*. What? You're shitting me...

- Exhibit more patience when dealing with people who obviously have their heads up their asses.

- Be a better husband and father as soon as I remarry and start a new family.

- Try to get through an entire episode of anything produced by Tyler Perry.

- Slap the next person who says, "Oh, I don't follow the news."

- Embrace the fact that I'm well into middle age and stop trying to appear cool in front of the youngsters, yo' hashtag.

- Take all the energy I waste hating on Oprah and transfer it to Katie Couric.

- Exercise more. Step 1: take the batteries out of the remote.

- Eat better. And by "better," I mean "more" and "faster."

- Stop referring to sleep as "downtime."

- Work smarter, not harder. Step 1: Get a job with dumber people.

- Stop and smell the roses. Walk around me, asshole!

- Learn to read music rather than always waiting for the record to come out.

- Be thankful for small mercies, but really wallow in others' discomfort.

- Stop telling Carol, "This vacuum SUCKS!" and then breaking into laughter.

- Accept the things I cannot change, have the courage to change the things I can, and acquire the wisdom to know the difference between "No Standing" and "No Parking."

- Think globally, act locally. Step 1: Is there a touring company of *Les Miz* anywhere near here?

Second Chances

Someone once said, "You don't get a second chance to make a first impression."
The fact that we don't know who said that is proof-positive.

Call me Ishmael. Do not text for it costs me extra.

It is a truth universally acknowledged, that a single man in possession of a good fortune, must be in want of a wife. So insists the Chief Justice of the state of Alabama.

Happy families are all alike; every unhappy family is unhappy in its own way. But your mother takes things to a whole new level.

riverrun, past Eve and Adam's, from swerve of shore to bend of bay, brings us by a commodius vicus of recirculation back to Howth Castle and Environs. spellcheck useless.

It was the best of times, it was the worst of times, it was the age of wisdom, it was the age of foolishness, it was the epoch of belief, it was the epoch of incredulity, it was the season of Light, it was the season of Darkness, it was the spring of hope, it was the winter of despair. But enough about me – how was your day?

I am an invisible man. Please "like" me on Facebook.

Someone must have slandered Josef K., for one morning, without having done anything truly wrong, he was arrested. He lived in Ferguson, Missouri.

The sun shone, having no alternative, on the nothing new. I'm no scientist, but this seems to disprove your claims of "climate change."

If you really want to hear about it, the first thing you'll probably want to know is where I was born, and what my lousy childhood was like, and how my parents were occupied and all before they had me, and all that David Copperfield kind of crap, but I don't feel like going into it, if you want to know the truth. Didn't you read my online dating profile before sending me a wink?

It was a dark and stormy night; the rain fell in torrents, except at occasional intervals, when it was checked by a violent gust of wind which swept up the streets (for it is in London that our scene lies), rattling along the house-tops, and fiercely agitating the scanty flame of the lamps that struggled against the darkness. I'll be back with tomorrow's forecast after this commercial break.

It was a wrong number that started it, the telephone ringing three times in the dead of night, and the voice on the other end asking for someone he was not. This "Do Not Call" list is worthless.

Mother died today. The guilt-tripping ends.

He was an old man who fished alone in a skiff in the Gulf Stream and he had gone eighty-four days now without taking a fish. Still, it was better than any eighty-four days he'd ever spent at the office.

It was a pleasure to burn. That's the last John Grisham novel I'll ever buy.

In my younger and more vulnerable years my father gave me some advice that I've been turning over in my mind ever since. He said I shouldn't overthink things.

It was a queer, sultry summer, the summer they electrocuted the Rosenbergs, and I didn't know what I was doing in New York. Other than of course denying I'd ever known the Rosenbergs.

I was the shadow of the waxwing slain By the false azure in the windowpane; Surrounded by despair and gloom Trapped in my doctor's waiting room.

The towers of Zenith aspired above the morning mist; austere towers of steel and cement and limestone, sturdy as cliffs and delicate as silver rods. Ah, there's a Starbucks!

All this happened, more or less. Says Brian Williams.

Ten Reasons Not To Own Cats

I'm sure most of you know I was, for many years, the co-parent of five cats, all of whom were rescued in one way or another: shelter, stray, "foster home." (At the time this book is being published, we're down to three due to what we insist were "natural causes.")

Just some words of warning, based on what feels like several lifetimes of experience.

1. They like to share their food -- about 30 minutes after the digestive process has gotten underway.

2. They shed hair that finds its way into folded clothes underneath other folded clothes inside a chest of drawers behind closet doors. In other people's houses.

3. They like to keep you company, even when you are sleeping. Sometimes they offer you a "snack" in the middle of the night.

4. They lick and kiss and caress you right up until the moment they sink their needle-sharp claws deep into your soft, supple skin.

5. When company comes to call, they make a bee-line for the lap of the person who is most allergic to them.

6. They have boundary issues -- primarily with the sides of the litter pan, at which they aim their pee just slightly above.

7. When you get up from your favorite chair or spot on the couch, even for just a moment, you'll find them fast asleep in that very spot upon your return. When you try to reclaim it, they'll sink their needle-sharp claws deep into your soft, supple skin.

8. When they're not eating, they're thinking about eating and letting you know how hungry they are.

9. Whoever said "let sleeping dogs lie" obviously never owned a cat. Claws, skin, etc.

10. The difference between "kittens" and "cats" is like the difference between Lindsay Lohan in The Parent Trap and Lindsay Lohan in Liz & Dick.

Becoming a Regular Fixture

We made our way back to the lake house after that gut-wrenching closing at the end of May, finally taking spiritual as well as legal possession of it.

One week of renovations down -- a lifetime to go...

We are just back from spending our first week at the lake house. Some of our friends and family know the back story, and for those who don't I'll provide the quickest possible summary of the closing: in one day we became both homeowners and landlords. This was because the seller decided that the closing, contractually scheduled to occur on May 31st, wasn't gonna happen despite lack of any notification to the contrary from the buyers, or title company, or mortgage broker, or bank, or carpet cleaners or anybody involved with the transaction. Skipping forward a few harrowing hours, the seller finally agreed to pay us 3 days' rent to stay in the house until the following Monday and put up a security deposit just in case, in his then-haste to vacate, he busted something up. (And by "seller" I mean his real estate agent, who wrote two checks from his own personal account to cover the rent and security and asked us not to mention anything about it in front of his client once we finally all sat down together to complete the closing, due to the client's "anger management issues.")

So, we bought a house we couldn't move in to, at least not immediately, and therefore regrouped and on the next Friday picked up a trusty U-Haul trailer to take additional stuff we wanted to move into the new house. Those of you who have driven with a trailer hitched to the back of your vehicle know the feeling that comes over you: a sense of adventure; the rush of testosterone enhanced by the anticipation that the rear bumper of the car will rip free while on the highway, strewing your belongings all over the road and watching your wife's grandmother's antique chifferobe smashed into a thousand pieces by the 18-wheeler that's been dogging you since you're heeding the backwards sticker on the trailer fender warning HPM 22 DEEPS XAM (fender view).

My son and I picked up the trailer, parking it in our next-door neighbor/landlord's driveway. This was a kind gesture on our landlord's part, particularly since a week before our closing he informed us we'd need to move out of our apartment since his son needed to move in. It's a long story and not germane to the current narrative, so I'll skip ahead about 10 minutes to when we started to load the trailer, which of course is when it began to pour.

We got almost everything loaded that we wanted to take up for this first trip (trailer was packed pretty tightly and so no room for the Weber grill or the box of toothpicks) and had a largely sway-free drive up to the house. Fortunately, we arrived ahead of the storm front and managed to get everything inside before the rains caught up with us again and decided to hang around there for the rest of our week at the lake.

The guy we bought the house from, in addition to being a COMPLETE FUCKING ASSHOLE (I'm back to the closing/rental situation again; sorry) was a very heavy smoker. When we first viewed the house, his agent cleverly attempted to disguise the lingering odor with a nifty little portable convection oven he'd set up to produce freshly-baked apple turnovers, along with one of those pod coffee makers so we could have a cup of... whatever comes out of those pod coffee makers to accompany our warm, scented pastry. But, being the sensitive-nosed types we are, we knew the smoke was going to be an issue. Therefore we arranged for a local fellow to come in with his environmentally-friendly set up and clean the carpets, walls and ceilings to remove the smell. (I would rate the ciggie smell as about 8.5 out of 10 -- 9 would be if the seller were still in the house, blowing smoke directly into our faces, and 10 is when you're trapped in a tobacco barn fire with no means of escape.) The enviro-treatment was partially successful, dialing the smell down to around a 3 or 4. That was still pretty strong and in fact Carol and I stopped at CVS for a couple boxes of nicotine patches to slap on so we wouldn't suffer withdrawal when leaving the house. Each day we reduced the smell a bit more, slapping on one less patch, cleaning in all those nooks and crannies that make English muffins so appealing but house cleaning such drudgery.

We were at the house from that Friday afternoon until the following Sunday, working very hard and enjoying occasional views of the lake in between cloudbursts. We saw lots of wildlife - a beaver, a woodpecker, bullfrogs, a loon (the seller's cousin, perhaps?), an osprey, a variety of finches and robins, and a chick on the back of a Harley. Our meticulous, relentless approach to cleaning removed all lingering traces of our interest in cleaning anything ever again. Other highlights from the week:

- Carol was anxious to get started with painting, and waited only an hour after starting to cut in the kitchen ceiling to ask me how she should cut in the kitchen ceiling. I yelled at her and as a result she did an excellent job disregarding my instructions. The kitchen ceiling she painted turned out beautifully; the bathroom ceiling I painted looked like I'd swiped at it with a rag while passing by on a roller coaster. (Hey, I made a joke there -- "roller" coaster!)

- We bought several ceiling fans to replace the crud-and-smoke encrusted ones already hanging in the house. Don't be fooled by those brands trumpeting "Five-Minute Installation" -- the small print says "after making electrical connections." I now know why they call it a "ground wire" -- forget to connect it to that little green screw and, once you flip the switch, you'll be six feet under before you know it.

- We bought a couch that almost fit through the doorway.

- We thought we'd solve the dilemma presented by an off-center fixture in the kitchen by installing track lighting. Three trips to the store, a call to Home Depot's customer service hotline, one defective unit, several dropped screws and nine-hours-spread-over-two-days later -- it's beautiful!

- The light kit had by far the worst set of installation instructions I'd ever come across. It wasn't so much the "English as written by the Chinese" syntax as the fact that individual parts were referred to with multiple names throughout: the same piece was called a "canopy," a "mounting cover," a "mounting plate," and an "end connector." To that list, I also added "this fucking piece of shit."

- Despite Carol's concern for critters, there is no such thing as a "catch and release" ant trap.

- If you knock over an open gallon of paint, you might as well sell the house at a distressed price and move elsewhere.

- Removing tub grout is a relatively easy job. Doing so without gouging the walls and tub surround, not so much.

- Shopping at the community hardware store that's been in business since forever is a great way to support the local economy especially since you'll pay three times what everything costs at the national chains.

- Soft-serve ice cream heals all hurt feelings.

We'll be heading up several more times over the next few weeks to finish painting, install more fixtures, and hack away at overgrown shrubbery within which we suspect the seller may now be living. We'll continue working as a team on renovating our dream house.

And eating lots more soft-serve.

Cause for Alarm

Years ago I had a laser printer. One morning, in the middle of printing a multi-page document, I heard a woman's voice, clear as a bell and seemingly right behind me, say "Your printer is out of toner." I just about jumped out of my skin thinking someone had crept into the house (and for some reason express an unusual interest in my toner level) until I heard it again and realized it was a notification coming from the printer via the computer speakers. It was completely natural-sounding; nothing HAL 9000-like or with the awkward cadence of the GPS lady giving you directions.

I no longer have that laser printer. I tell people it's because a replacement toner cartridge cost more than a brand-new ink-jet printer. But the real reason is because I believed the printer was possessed, and I didn't want to run the risk of reaching for a document and having a hand come out of the discharge tray and reach for me.

Carol and I were just about to step out of the house to head for a Sunday morning hike when the smoke alarm went off. In between a series of 85-decibel warning shrieks the downstairs unit frantically shouted "FIRE!! FIRE!!" just in case we didn't get the point. With no apparent signs of smoke I pushed a button to trigger the "hush" feature, which is there in case I've merely burned the toast or decided to take up smoking cigars indoors. We have three inter-connected units and by now the other two had taken up the war cry, so I dashed around the house to get them all to shut the   £#¢k up. Presuming the source has been contained within ten minutes, the system will then reset and remain silent. During that time, I checked to make sure all the appliances were off (they were) and then wedged myself into the crawl space under the house to see if the oil burner was engulfed in flames (it wasn't). Finding no apparent source of concern I came back inside, expecting the incident to become a distant if unsettling memory. Presuming this had been just an anomalous outburst, we picked up our hiking supplies and headed again for the door.

Right at the ten-minute mark: "SHRIEK - SHRIEK - SHRIEK!!" "FIRE!! FIRE!!" "SHRIEK - SHRIEK - SHRIEK!!" "WARNING!! CARBON MONOXIDE!!" That was a new wrinkle -- invisible, deadly gas was now potentially introduced into the alleged calamity. I mashed the hush buttons again but none of the units would stop screaming. Besides the two of us going deaf, the poor cats were completely freaked out and ran around the house seeking refuge from the noise. I opened the door to the electrical panel and flipped off the breaker controlling the alarms. That didn't faze them since there is also a 9-volt battery in each unit as a backup. I popped open the door to the battery compartments to completely disconnect the power. Even then, the system made a gasp with its last breath, sounding like someone in the midst of an asthma attack gasping in a hoarse whisper for an inhaler just out of reach. "Shriek!... shriek... fi..re.."

By now we were thoroughly rattled and decided to put off our departure until we could get the alarms to calm down permanently. I dug out the user's guide and spent a solid fifteen minutes trying to make sense of it. With a collapsed size the same as a deck of playing cards, and seemingly contrary to the dictum that no piece of paper can be folded in half more than seven times, the fully expanded guide ended up hanging over the edges of our dining room table. I finally found the troubleshooting section after trying to read type set with a font size of "neutrino." Here I was instructed to remove the units from their wall mounts and give them a thorough vacuuming to remove any dust. I did so, then remounted them and flipped on the breaker. While this effort seemed to soothe the upstairs hallway alarm, the other two immediately resumed their overlapping hyperbole, creating a ping-ponging echo between upstairs and down: "WARNING!!NING!! CARBONBON MONOXIDE!!NOXIDE!!" Now we were convinced the alarms were dysfunctional and so left for our stroll with the breaker shut off, batteries disconnected... and windows open. Just in case.

Every few months there's a story on the news about an electrical fire where overheated wiring buried in a wall smolders for hours before finally combusting. The unsuspecting family returns home several hours later to find their house engulfed in flames and all their belongings reduced to ash.

That's not at all what happened to us -- but I had you there for a moment, didn't I? The house was intact and the cats were roaming around, still suffering with tinnitus but conscious and alert -- so no fire and no gas leak. I replaced the units the next day, opting to go with a system that was not interconnected. So far we haven't been startled by any further digitized warning cries. Or tripped over any dead cats. Everything is back to normal and we're again tripping over the cats only when they're sleeping on the stairs. I guess the next thing I need to install is a "lack of motion" detector in order to avoid a completely different kind of cat-tastrophe.

I hope that feeble pun didn't alarm you.

Prattle of the Sexes

When Carol and I were planning our wedding, I told her that she shouldn't feel obligated to take my last name. In fact, I would be willing to take her last name if she so requested.

She looked at me like I was an idiot and said, "What kind of an idiot are you?"

I like to think we have always had a contemporary relationship, not mired in traditional gender-based roles. I like to think that.

She says: "Maybe your brother can give you a hand while he's here."

She means: "You have made a complete mess of this project, you fucking idiot. Fix it."

He says: "Go ahead, suit yourself."

He means: "I am paying absolutely no attention to what you just said."

She says: "I'd like some more help around the house."

She means: "I met with a divorce attorney today."

He says: "You look great!"

He means: "Get in the car already."

She says: "Is that what you're wearing?"

She means: "How old were you when your mother stopped dressing you - 23?"

He says: "You don't have to come if you don't want to."

He means: "Please please please please don't come with me; it's emasculating."

She says: "That was nice."
She means: "Nice try."

He says: "That was nice."
He means: "I'm going to sleep now."

She says: "I'll just be a minute in this store."
She means: "You might as well take a nap on a bench in the food court."

He says: "We can't afford it."
He means: "Unless I give up my dream of buying a boat."

She says: "Dinner was delicious!"
She means: "Nice try."

He says: "Dinner was delicious!"
He means: "If I keep complimenting you, hopefully I'll never have to cook again."

She says: "It wasn't that expensive."
She means: "Compared to the price of a boat."

He says: "I can't imagine my life without you and the kids."
He means: "I can't take care of myself."

She says: "I can't imagine my life without you and the kids."
She means: "Well, without the kids."

He says: "I love you."

He means: "I hope you won't be too mad when you see our new boat parked in the driveway."

She says: "I love you."

She means: "In spite of your many flaws."

Storm (Door) Chasers

Happy Fourth of July! We've moved the celebration up a day in the Boston area due to an impending storm passing through tomorrow. I plan to get a ballot initiative underway to have Christmas celebrated the day after Thanksgiving -- you're already suffering with your family that Thursday so why not just stick it out another day rather than having to go through it all over again in another month?

As you may already know, home improvement projects and I get along like Rush Limbaugh and anyone with a lick of common sense. Nevertheless, I keep taking these challenges on and they keep challenging me back.

We were up at the lake last weekend and stopped at Home Depot to pick up a variety of items, including a storm door so we could leave the back door open and let those lovely lake breezes blow all the way through the house. As with everything you go to purchase at a "big box" store, there aren't just a few options to choose from; there are dozens of choices to confound you. Storm doors fall right in-line – I'd say there were between 15-20 distinct models (excluding various sizes and colors) with varying arrays of features. With assistance from an exceedingly pleasant employee, we narrowed down our semi-finalists to 3 different doors.

[Quick aside: Almost to a fault, we've found retail employees up in Maine to be painfully patient and helpful. Having lived in several large metropolitan areas over the years, we've become accustomed to and almost expect some degree of resentfulness / confrontation / disinterest from a fair percentage of those making a living in the service trades, but when dealing with Mainers we've been knocked off-balance by their kind and genuine approach to dealing with the public.]

[Aside to the above aside: We needed the services of a plumber over the winter and, while the work was quite competently done, it took a long time to make the arrangements to get the repairs underway and almost as long afterwards to get the office to provide an invoice. Everything was handled over the phone or via email, and I mailed house keys for the plumber's use. When we finally returned to our home post-repairs I drove over to the plumber's place of business to retrieve my keys, meeting him in-person for the first time. We had a pleasant conversation and I mentioned that I'd like to pay for the services rendered but hadn't yet received a bill from his office manager/wife Cindy. He said, "Oh, don't worry – we'll get it to ya' soon enough. Cindy's been on screech all winter long." I nodded my head in agreement but had no idea what it meant to be "on screech?" She'd spent the winter huddled in a Snuggie, watching reruns of *Saved By The Bell*? Had stopped taking her Xanax? Was committed to intense owl-watching? Fast-forward to this past weekend and Carol ended up calling Cindy about an unrelated matter and had the presence of mind to ask for clarification: "on screech" is a Maine-ism for "full-out busy." Linguistic mystery solved!]

So, picking up where I left off... We narrowed it down to 3 different doors, finally selecting one that had a half-screen that slid out of view and was in the middle of the price range. Our very helpful employee immediately offered to grab a dolly cart, pull and load the door on it, and walk it to the front of the store for checkout. What a guy! We paid for our purchases; I rolled the door outside; Carol went to get the car, and yet another unnaturally-helpful employee came out to tie the door up on the luggage rack for the trip home.

The next morning I woke up early and decided to get started on the installation before it got too hot outside (temps were going to be in the high 80s). I carefully opened the door-sized cardboard box to reveal the contents and there I saw – the wrong door. It was a full-screen model with a replaceable full-glass insert (vs. the nifty hidden half-screen door we'd chosen). I taped the box back together, tied it up on the luggage rack, and made the 20-mile trip back to Home Depot. I ended up dealing with the same "helpful" employee who'd sold us the door; he was apologetic, selected the correct door, and with a little prompting from me offered an additional discount to compensate for the inconvenience. Checkout; load up; drive back home again.

Now, instead of an early-morning start it was approaching high noon. I started over again, carefully opening the box so I didn't damage its contents. I began to read the directions and was confounded almost immediately. The first step was to attach a long "z-bar" that had the door's hinges as its integral part. The directions said to place the z-bar in an orientation that would line up the bottom hole in the top-most hinge with a pre-drilled hole in the frame and then insert a screw. I managed to do that (aren't you proud of me?) and was now instructed to insert seven more screws to secure all the hinges to the door. But – where were the other seven holes? Only that first one was pre-existing and the instructions said nothing about prepping for the others (later steps were explicit about making center punches and drilling pilot holes before inserting the screws). I puzzled over this for a good 10-15 minutes before appealing to a higher authority – the missus. Carol came out to take a look and was as befuddled as I. She's got a master's degree, so... It wasn't just me. I ended up looking at a video online and that's when I finally discovered the hinge screws were "self-tapping." In case you don't know, that means no pilot holes need to be drilled; just start a-screwin' and they'll work their way through the sheet metal.

Well, fer Crissakes – why didn't they just SAY this in the directions? And why weren't ALL the screws required for this installation self-tapping? I'm sure there's a reason for this that my contracting or engineering friends can validate but don't confuse me with the facts here.

With minimal mis-steps the installation continued apace... well, I should say at a pace leading to its completion a mere five hours after I started (the second time). Miraculously, the door was square in the frame; it swung closed and latched nearly every time; the cool hidden screen worked like it was supposed to; I was only suffering mildly from heat stroke, and I had only a few random parts left over. We'll have to wait for the first rain to make sure it's watertight but so far, so good. One of the selling points of this model was its "oops-proof" guarantee – any parts damaged during installation would be replaced free of charge. The downside of this model is that the half-screen scrolls down to the level of the door handle, so I fear someone is going to try to push on the "door" and instead punch a palm through the irreplaceable screen section.

Once that happens you'll hear me "on screech" -- all the way from the Maine interior.

The Right to Bare Arms

There's nothing funny about guns, nothing at all. And while there may be opportunities to exploit amusing aspects of gun ownership or regulation, I think it's probably not a good idea to ridicule a gun owner since they may not see the same humor in the situation that I do. I'd especially avoid teasing in a "concealed carry" situation.

I was shot in the workplace the other day by someone who didn't know how to properly use a gun. This really happened.

Granted, it was a Nerf gun shooting a foam-bodied projectile with a plastic tip -- but it still hurt like hell. My "friend" (ha!) at work picked up the Nerf gun, which was lying on top of a small storage cabinet between my desk and my neighbor's, and started to play with it while waiting for me to finish an email before heading out together for a coffee break. I was focused on my desktop monitor and suddenly SMACK!!! The Nerf projectile struck me in the side of my neck. It had been "accidentally" (ha!) fired about 18 inches away from my head. My "friend" (ha!) shrieked in dismay once the weapon discharged, and I let loose with a series of expletives that would surely land me a part in the next Martin Scorsese movie.

The perpetrator (new name for my "friend") apologized profusely and then offered the following excuses:

- "I was just playing around with it."

- "I didn't know it was loaded."

- "I didn't know how to operate it properly."

- "I never fired a Nerf gun before."

- "It shouldn't have been out in the open."

- "You were sitting too close to it when it went off."

OK, that last one I made up but the perp rattled off all the rest of them. The shooter attempted to absolve herself of any personal responsibility for the situation, so blaming the victim was sure to be next in her series of disingenuous statements if we hadn't already made it to the coffee shop by then. There was a quick reference to how she'd "Dick Cheney'd" me, alluding to the former Vice President's hunting accident some years back where he blasted a companion with a load of buckshot. If you recall, the victim in that shooting later apologized to Cheney, saying he was sorry "for all that Vice President Cheney and his family [had] to go through." Well, I'm not planning to apologize to my assailant, that's for sure.

Plus, the only thing my family had to endure were spasms of laughter when I told them I'd been shot with a Nerf.

Sick of It All

The other afternoon I ran into a co-worker taking a break in our employee cafeteria. He was reading a book and said it was so interesting he didn't want to stop to go back to work. I suggested he should call out "engrossed" the next day so he could finish it.

That got me thinking about some excuses we could start beta testing since "I'm sick" has been done to death (no pun intended). Let me know if any of the suggestions below work for you:

- "My cat is pregnant and I'm her doula."

- "I'm binge-watching *The Sopranos* and will be in as soon as I see who walks into the diner."

- "I'm in the hospital. Well, I'm in the hospital gift shop."

- "I finished all my work yesterday. What -- there's more?"

- "I'm waiting to get my mojo back."

- "I've got *Do You Believe* by Cher stuck in my head and really shouldn't come in until it works its way back out."

- "I'm on a medication that advises against operating heavy machinery, and I really don't know how much my computer weighs."

- "I got my mojo back but it turned out to be somebody else's... Still waiting for mine."

- "I ran out of pre-tax transportation credits and have to wait for the next pay period before I can reload my transit pass."

- "Our CEO told me over drinks last night I could take the rest of the week off."

- "My car died and I'm in mourning."

- "When I left yesterday I said, 'See you tomorrow' and you said 'Not if I see you first', so I thought we were playing 'Hide-and-Seek' today."

- "I've lost interest in what we do. But please call me if anything new comes up."

- "I had such a productive day yesterday that any effort I might make today would only pale by comparison."

- "My work-life balance is out of whack and I'll be away from the office until equilibrium is restored."

- "Instead of coming in and waiting to get paid, I'd prefer to get paid first and then I'll think about coming in."

- "I see nothing to be gained by returning to that hellhole. I think the real question is why you still work there."

Speaker of the House

I used to be pretty good, or at least consistently average, at installing and maintaining the various "devices" around the house -- computer, TV, audio, etc.

Now, however, I'm beginning to respond more often to offers including "free installation." Especially since I've noticed, more and more, that the new stuff no longer comes with much in the way of instructions -- relying instead on drawings with little or no verbiage -- to allegedly walk you through the set-up process. I may be a visual learner but even I have my limits.

Proof thereof:

Cruising through one of the big warehouse stores while waiting for the missus to decide on a pair of glasses, I spied a wireless TV soundbar on markdown. "I've got to have that," I convinced myself. I had a $10 gift card burning a hole in my wallet, making it an even more appealing deal, so when we walked out of the store my wife held a receipt for the promise of her new glasses in three weeks while I had a brand new toy to play with that very afternoon. I won.

Until I got home and unpacked my purchase. I'm not sure how "wireless" made it into the product description since the first step in the instructions was to plug the speaker into an outlet. I'm no electrician, but I believe that requirement exposed the "wireless" designation as a bald-faced lie. Step 2 was to establish the "wireless" connection between the soundbar and TV set. O... K... I guess that's what they were referring to on the package description. The soundbar and our TV were from the same manufacturer and the instructions indicated that any set produced by the company since 2012 had this feature built in to facilitate such a set up. I'd purchased our set in late 2013, right after we'd moved into our lake house, so I figured I was good to go. I figured wrong.

The TV did not have the "Sound Connect" feature as part of its array. Now I had to default to an alternate installation option, which specified the use of an "AUX Cable (not supplied)." Are you freaking KIDDING ME? After briefly flipping out, I noticed there was an optic cable included with the speaker which could be used as an alternate to the alternate. Huzzah.

Now all that was left to do was place the battery in the remote control (another remote control to add to my already impressive collection) and turn this sucker on. I pressed the power button and nothing happened. I continued to press the button, adding the "extend arm toward the device, using the elbow" motion as if I just needed to give the infrared impulse a little push to get it close enough to be recognized by the unit. Still no luck. I thought perhaps the battery was dead. Luckily I happened to have the same kind of pancake-shaped power source in my odds and ends box, so I swapped it out and tried again. Same outcome as Nixon's assessment of the results of the ten-year air campaign during the Vietnam War: "Zilch." I walked over and pressed the manual power switch built into the front of the console; the display lit up and a few seconds later sound issued from the speaker. Utilizing my acute knowledge of home sound system manufacturing processes I deduced the remote was defective. Crap.

Seeking a replacement, I called the manufacturer's toll-free customer service number and connected with a live representative after a shockingly minimal amount of menu navigation. The agent was very pleasant, empathizing with my issue and assuring me she could help resolve the matter quickly. She told me to remove the battery and then repeatedly press as many buttons on the remote as I could. I responded by assuring her I felt confident I could press all of the buttons -- no technical novice was I. After doing so, she told me to reinsert the battery. Then she asked if I had a camera nearby -- ??? Or did my smartphone have a camera built in -- ??? Confused, I said my phone had a camera, whereupon she told me to point the remote at the phone while in camera mode and then press the power button. Ah, now I understood -- this was a way for me to see if it was working without being blinded by whatever kind of pulse emanated from the device. I confirmed I saw flashing via the camera display, which pleased the rep. "Great!" she exclaimed. "Now we have confirmed that your remote is functioning properly. This means the receptor on your soundbar is defective. You can return it to our service center to have it repaired." I replied since I'd purchased the unit mere hours before I would instead return it to the store for an exchange. Annoying, but quicker and easier than repackaging the unit, mailing it back to the company and waiting weeks for its return.

Carol had been seated at the computer this whole time, close enough to hear the troubleshooting discussion. Once I'd hung up the phone and expressed my dismay at having purchased a bum speaker, she got up without a word and walked over to where I'd set it up in front of the TV. Giving it a quick once-over, she lifted up the speaker and rotated it 90 degrees on its horizontal axis before setting it back down. "Try the remote again," she commanded. Shaking my head to imply "Whatever..." I pressed the button and the speaker immediately lit up. Speaking the words I was too dumbstruck to voice myself, Carol clarified I'd placed the speaker with its grill facing down rather than facing out from the TV (the manual controls were now displayed on the top, rather than the front, of the unit). Once the grill was in the correct alignment the sensor was exposed, and everything worked as it should.

Except, of course, for my brain. That unit remains defective and, sadly, is long out of warranty.

Step Aside

If you haven't come to visit us up at the lake, you are welcome to do so.

If you bring smallish children, that's fine. We'll ask you to sign a waiver agreeing to abide by "house rules." Mom and Dad (or Same Sex Parent #2; we're inclusive) can head out in the kayaks for a relaxing afternoon on the water and when you come back -- you'll hardly recognize the little bastar... uh, your progeny.

Friends came for a recent visit with their two adorable daughters, ages 3 and 1.5, in tow. The kids were bright, energetic, charming and maddening -- usually all at once. While Carol and I are creeping up on our 60s (well, I am -- Carol appears to be holding steady at 35), we have a number of friends we consider "young marrieds," many of whom have children who are at or below kindergarten age. We love being referred to as "Aunt Carol" and "Uncle John" (if our friends weren't flattering us by encouraging the kids to call us by those titles, "Grandma Carol" and "Pa-Pa John" would be more accurate) and do our best to be the kind of up-for-anything and cuddly faux-relatives all youngsters should have in their lives.

Except when the kids do something to piss us off. Then the laughter and popsicles and gentle sing-song voices quickly disappear and we become crotchety and irritable. Books being read from are snapped shut. Smiles turn to scowls. Fun and games becomes "Law & Order." We try very hard to refrain from getting involved in disciplining other people's children -- that's their parents' job, and our various friends really do have a great handle on raising their kids with the right mix of encouragement, boundary setting and age-appropriate discipline. But sometimes something happens and we just... can't... help ourselves. Carol is big on table manners: "Don't play with your food," "No dessert until you eat your vegetables," that kind of thing. I exercised restraint during several parent-and-child standoffs until I ducked barefoot into our bathroom after coming in from the lake and stepped on some little person's turd.

"WHO WAS JUST IN THE BATHROOM?? WHO USED THE TOILET LAST??" I calmly inquired as I strode out, using just the heel of one foot. My questions were met by startled expressions and silence. "WHO WAS IN THERE BEFORE ME??" I rephrased.

"I STEPPED ON A PIECE OF SHI... er, there was POOP ON THE FLOOR!!" If neither of the children had gone Number Two previously, they surely had a strong urge to now.

The younger one is still in diapers, so the only viable suspects were her older sister or one of our cats. The cats spent most of our friends' visit hiding under the beds upstairs, preferring to remain as far from the strangers in their house as the floor plan would allow. It was entirely possible one of the cats might have dragged a "deposit" from the litter box to another location. However, as a long-time cat owner, I have a pretty discriminating eye and can distinguish between human and feline scat. This was people-poop stuck to the arch of my right foot.

Inexplicably, both girls began to cry as though they'd been subjected to a grueling interrogation rather than simply asked to confirm their recent presence in the loo. Carol gave me her "See what you've done?" look while their parents exchanged embarrassed glances and rushed to check for soiled diapers and underwear along with any other evidence of errant excretions. While I felt my response had been quite temperate under the circumstances (hey -- do you speak in calm and measured tones after stepping in shit?), I tried to reset the tone by shouting merrily above the resulting fray, "WHO'S READY FOR SOME ICE CREAM?!"

Just that quickly, I'd stepped in it again.

Rage Against the Washing Machine

"If your only tool is a hammer, then every problem looks like a nail."

To that I say: "If you have a box full of tools, then you've got a shitload of problems to deal with."

If you ever move next door to me and need some help with an around-the-home project, you'll be better served by asking your neighbor on the other side. I am incompetent when it comes to tools and anything smacking of fix-it. Some folks quaintly refer to the husband's "honey-do" list; mine is a "honey, for God's sake please don't" list.

- Carpentry? I'll cut the boards too short and get splinters.

- Plumbing? Have plenty of towels on hand to sop up the flowing water.

- Car repair? Make sure you've got a bus schedule handy.

- Painting? As long as you're not fussy about color, coverage or completion – I'm your guy. But I hate to paint, so there's that.

Buying our home up at the lake last year has provided me with multiple opportunities to display my general contracting incompetence. We've had tons of projects to complete and I've done an exemplary job at none of them. A man's reach should exceed his grasp, and I'm reaching for marginal. Most recently I attempted to repair our washing machine. SPOILER ALERT: there are puddles involved.

Our pipes froze and burst this winter. That's another long story. Actually, it isn't: our pipes froze and burst this winter -- The End. That led to damage in the water lines, the heat registers, the toilet, the kitchen sink and the washing machine. We had a plumber come in who handled the first four but for reasons unknown doesn't *do* washing machine repair. He did, however, remove the lid to take a look-see and let me know the inlet valve was cracked. For those of you unfamiliar with washing machine construction, that's the part into which you screw the hoses from the water supply. There are electrical connections so the machine knows if you've requested cold, hot or warm water for the wash. I went to the local appliance store in our small Maine town with the model and serial numbers for our washer, and the nice man behind the counter scrounged up the appropriately-sized replacement. I asked if I could arrange a service visit to get it installed... He laughed derisively and baited me by saying, "It's an easy job! You can do it yourself!" Before I could contradict him he pulled up a diagram of our washer on his computer, one of those pictures with all the parts exploded (how apt) into three dimensions so you can see what goes where. He pointed out the valve and said I just needed to "angle it" to get the old one out and new one in. Two screws held it in place, and one of them was "blind." This meant the screw was located on the underside of the valve assembly and it wasn't visible while trying to put it in or take it out. (There's a joke to be made here about blind screwing but I'll pass at this time.)

Despite my better judgment, I let myself get carried away by his cajoling and, box tucked under my arm, headed home, prepared to successfully complete this simple install. By the time I got back (10 minutes later), my commitment had waned sufficiently that I no longer felt confident in my ability and told Carol I'd decided to "wait for another day" to attempt the job.

That day came six weeks later.

Fortified by a large breakfast, several cups of coffee and at least one shot of Maker's Mark, I decided this was the time to tackle the task. I wrestled the washer out from its closet location far enough so I could squeeze in and line up behind the inlet valve. First screw out – no problem. "Blind" screw removal – big problem. Couldn't see it, couldn't reach it. Carol offered to give it a try.

Now, just because I'm incompetent doesn't mean I don't have feelings or an easily-bruised male ego... I politely (not really) rejected her first few offers and continued to express my mounting frustration in language I'll delicately describe as "colorful." Finally I agreed to swap places with Carol and she folded much faster than I had – couldn't see, couldn't reach, etc. We agreed I'd make an appointment for a service tech to come out some other time we'd be at the lake and take care of it.

That futile effort wasted nearly all of our Saturday morning. (Well, in the interest of accuracy I should mention I'd been up since

6:00 whereas Carol wandered downstairs closer to 11:00.) We made the most of the rest of a very pleasant day together by running errands, planting flowers, drinking beer, bird-watching, drinking gin and tonics, making pizza, drinking wine, and starting a fire (outdoors and intentionally). We went to bed still laundry-deprived and one of us might have been slightly hung over.

I woke up Sunday morning before Carol and slipped downstairs (literally – I slipped down the stairs; luckily they're carpeted) to make myself a badly-needed cup of coffee and enjoy the early-morning view of the lake. After a while I pulled out my tablet and found a video demonstrating the exact steps necessary to replace the inlet valve. It turns out the parts guy was correct about the "angle" but failed to mention there was a tube just to the right of the valve that should be removed to provide sufficient space to reach in and handle the blind screw and manipulate everything into place. I extracted the tube and -- Eureka! I was now able to exchange the old part for the new. I hooked up the electrical leads, replaced the tube, connected the hoses, put the top back on, wrestled the washer back into the closet and tested it out with a quick rinse cycle. Success! The machine worked AND I didn't see any water leaking.

Carol came downstairs and was thrilled I'd been able to snatch victory from the jaws of defeat. We washed one load of towels and declared we were satisfied with how the machine was operating.

After completing a few more errands, it was time for us to pack up and head back to Boston. I was about to get in the shower when Carol asked me if I needed "those two screws." I thought she was referring to the ones that went with the washer top; I couldn't find the originals but had two others in my toolbox and used them instead. I told her that and she replied, "OK… but aren't these the screws for the inlet valve?" Oh… shit. In my giddiness at successfully getting the part angled in, I'd forgotten all about actually securing it. After a brief but intense session of colorful language, I pulled out the washer, took off the lid, removed the tube, and tried to figure out how to get the blind screw in place. After 15 minutes and using every screwdriver and piece of cutlery at my disposal, I finally found something that gave me sufficient clearance to get my hand in to turn while keeping the screw aligned. As Carol said: "If a job's worth doing, it's worth doing three times." Truer words were never more deeply resented.

As I started to push the washer back into the closet, I noticed something – a puddle of water on the floor. The parts guy had mentioned that the drain pump might also have suffered a crack from the freeze, but since we didn't find any water underneath the machine when moving it out for the valve replacement I discounted that possibility (also because one of the two screws holding the kick panel in place, behind which the pump is located, was so badly stripped and rusted I couldn't get it out).

There's a video on YouTube showing what an "easy job" it is to replace the drain pump on a washing machine. You are welcome to search for it and if you agree we'll gladly provide you with overnight accommodations at the lake, some homemade pizza and up to two beers in return for your efforts. I'll send directions after I hear from you. By the way, Carol likes to sleep in so please keep any "colorful language" while you work to a minimum.

Road Hard, Put Away Wet

Virtually every little boy and girl (and, in the spirit of inclusiveness, every gender-fluid child) in our country dreams of growing up and becoming President one day. I have a message for the youngsters of our nation: it can happen for you -- because it happened to me.

Last Saturday, I was elected President. Granted, it was as the head of our local road association, but still... The title is "President" and I accepted the honor with grace and humility. That morning we held our annual association meeting; the vote in favor of my candidacy was unanimous. I suspect this is less a reflection of my popularity among my neighbors and more that no one else was remotely interested in the job. Nonetheless, it will make a nice accomplishment for my future biographer to highlight.

A neighbor down the street served as President for the last two years, but this year decided she was ~~fed up~~ had other interests to pursue and so declined another term in office. She called me a few weeks ago to ask if I would consider running for the job (I believe the actual request was: "Are you willing to do it? Because I sure as shit can't be bothered anymore."); if so, she would place my name in nomination. As flattered as I was, I still approached the opportunity with a level head and had a few questions for her:

- How much is the presidential stipend?

- Why is there no presidential stipend?

- Does the President have check-signing authority?

- Have the association's accounts ever been audited?

Once I felt I had a grasp of the position's parameters, I went about assembling my campaign team and preparing a press release announcing my candidacy. Much to my surprise, the so-called Mainstream Media had zero interest in covering the news. No reporters attended the rally I staged in my backyard, which meant I'd thrown two packs of hot dogs on the grill for naught. Come to think of it, I don't recall seeing any of my neighbors there, either. Our local ad-supported weekly publication said for a small fee they'd run a short write-up, so I emailed them the release. I was excited when I saw the article in print but was very disappointed when both my first and last names were misspelled. I contacted the editor, who told me that proofing cost extra. Sigh... Well, this was not a disaster on the level of Muskie bursting into tears back in '72 (which seems so quaint compared to what we witnessed in 2016, yes?), so I shook up the team (which, so far, was only my wife and myself -- and one of us had to go. Sorry, honey...) and pressed on.

I won't draw any comparisons between the 2016 campaign and my own, with this exception -- say what you want about the two major candidates and the election outcome, but regardless of party affiliation many folks say one flaw in Hillary's effort was that she came across as distant and remote, not embracing the kind of hands-on "retail politics" her husband Bill was famous for. I did not want to repeat that mistake, so I launched a walking tour to make the acquaintance of as many of my potential constituents as possible. There are only twenty houses on our road, and half of them aren't owner-occupied year-round, but that did not deter me from knocking on every door in an effort to hear from the community and present my case. I didn't take it personally when a few folks slammed their doors in my face, or when I clearly saw people through the screen sitting in their living rooms yet resolutely ignoring my "Hello?" -- but the third time someone sicced their dog on me, I decided my time was better spent disseminating my platform via social media.

Using several popular online platforms, I got an honest, unfiltered message out to my future ~~subjects~~ neighbors. They weren't much for the Twitter, but I did get quite a few comments in response to my Facebook posts. However, they were mostly links to cat videos or pictures of their grandchildren. A couple of them were videos of their grandchildren playing with cats.

I woke up early the morning of the association meeting and rehearsed my stump speech. As an effort to get out the vote, I brought travel-sized bottles of Maalox and Kaopectate to distribute. But, as I mentioned above, nearly all the preparation was rendered unnecessary since no opponent emerged to challenge me. Nonetheless, I was proud of the campaign I'd run: focused on the issues (well, just the one issue -- overseeing maintenance of the road), no negative messaging (instead of accusing anyone of exceeding the posted 15 MPH speed limit, I thanked everyone who honored the voluntary 8:30 PM curfew), with appeal to a broad demographic, which in this case was men and women, mostly retired, ages 60 to 85.

Now that the election is behind me -- the focus is on a future of leading with clear vision and a steady hand. Both of which will be necessary since I've just learned the Association's finances are in the red, so apparently I'm expected to use my snow blower to clear everyone's driveway this winter and also operate a grader to re-level the road once we get through next spring's mud season. My advice to those dreaming youngsters? Take your time, do your research, and make sure you understand the span of responsibilities you'll be expected to embrace. It would be devastating, in response to your decision to chase elective office, to have people accuse you of Russian into it.

Postface

Many thanks to the loyal blog readers who provided feedback and support prior to this publication. I appreciate the kind words of encouragement provided by all three of you.

None of this would have been possible without the life lived with, participation of and legal release signed by my lovely wife, Carol. Less than three (signed) Hub-bub.

If this book was too much for you, sorry. If it was just right, groovy. If it's left you hungry for more, there are additional blog posts from years past as well as newer entries available for your reading pleasure at JohnBranning.com.

Any praise or comments about this book or the blog, you are welcome to email to me at JohnBranning@yahoo.com. Any criticism you can keep to yourself. Or at least express with less profanity than I included in some of the material contained herein.

About the Author

Strewn about the author you'll find a variety of cats, cat toys, non-functioning electronic equipment and hairballs.

If you did not glean any of this from reading the book, John, his lovely wife Carol and their three remaining cats (Miles, Sophie and Nate -- short for "Concatenate") live on Annabessacook Lake in Winthrop, Maine. He is a former resident of Massachusetts, South Carolina, Maryland, New York State and Ontario, Canada and yet the process servers are somehow able to keep finding him.

John is approaching retirement age but emotionally remains in adolescence.

Carol and John have a grown son, Joshua, who lives in Boston and makes only a fleeting appearance in this book. The reasons for that may be disclosed in John's next book.